ROCK
GUITAR
BIBLE

HLE

Hal Leonard Europe
Distributed by Music Sales

Exclusive Distributors:
Music Sales Limited
8/9 Frith Street, London W1D 3JB, England.
Music Sales Pty Limited
120 Rothschild Avenue, Rosebery, NSW 2018, Australia.

Order No. HLE90001542
ISBN 0-7119-8734-3
This book © Copyright 2001 by Hal Leonard Europe

Printed in the USA
Cover design by Chloë Alexander

Your Guarantee of Quality
As publishers, we strive to produce every book to the highest
commercial standards.
The book has been carefully designed to minimise awkward page
turns and to make playing from it a real pleasure.
Throughout, the printing and binding have been planned to ensure a
sturdy, attractive publication which should give years of enjoyment.
If your copy fails to meet our high standards, please inform us and
we will gladly replace it.

Music Sales' complete catalogue describes thousands of titles and is
available in full colour sections by subject, direct from
Music Sales Limited. Please state your areas of interest and send a
cheque/postal order for £1.50 for postage to: Music Sales Limited,
Newmarket Road, Bury St. Edmunds, Suffolk IP33 3YB, England.

www.musicsales.com

CONTENTS

All Along the Watchtower

Words and Music by Bob Dylan

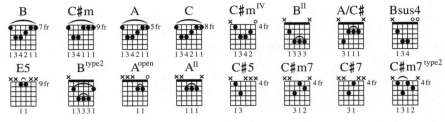

1.There must be some kind a way

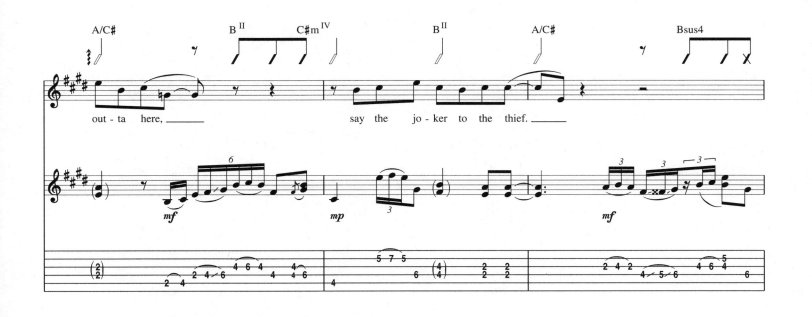

out-ta here, _____ say the jo-ker to the thief. _____

There's too much con-fu-sion, _____ na. I can't get no re-lief. ___

Busi-ness men, they ah, ah, drink my wine. _____

Plow man, dig my earth, _____ uh.   None _ will lev - el   on _

_ the line, _____ uh,   no - bod - y   of   it   is   worth. _   Hey, _____ hey! _

Guitar Solo

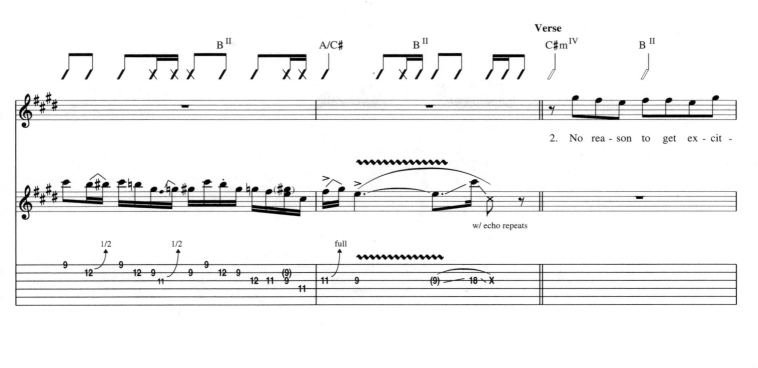

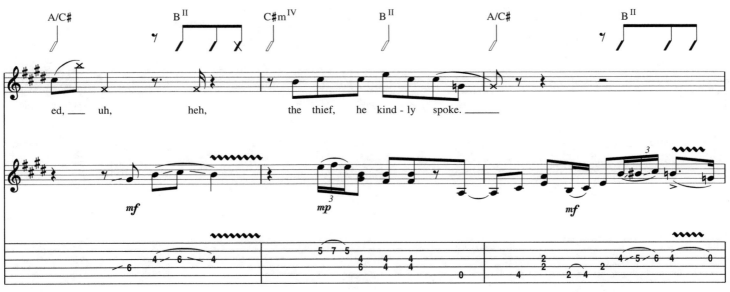

But uh, but you and I, we've been through that, but, ah, and this is not our fate.

So let us not talk false - ly now, the ho - ur's get-tin' late,

*Played ahead of the beat.

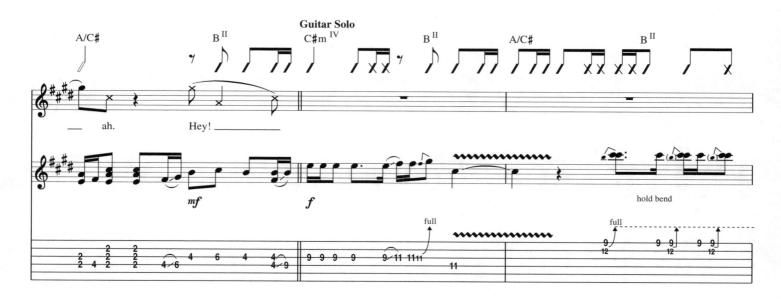

ah. Hey!

Guitar Solo

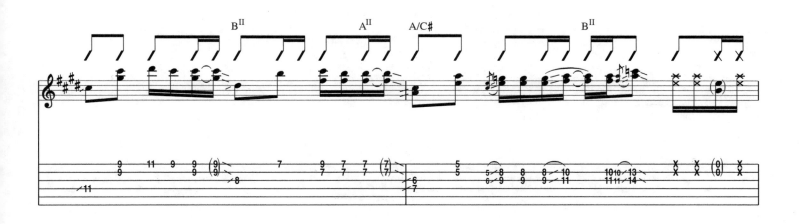

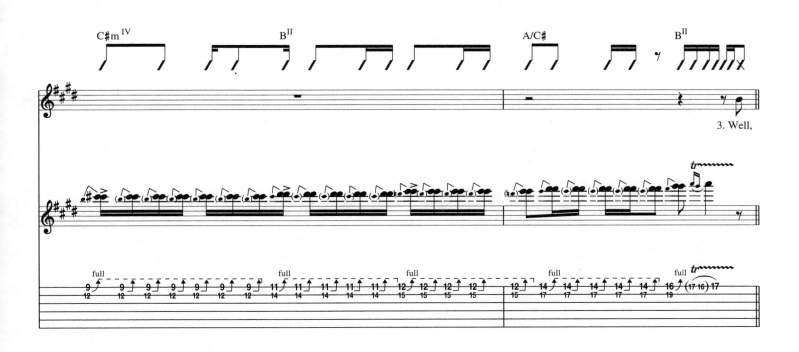

3. Well,

all a - long _ the watch - tow-er,   prin-ces   kept the   view. _

All Day and All of the Night

Words and Music by Ray Davies

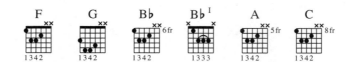

All Right Now

Words and Music by Paul Rodgers and Andy Fraser

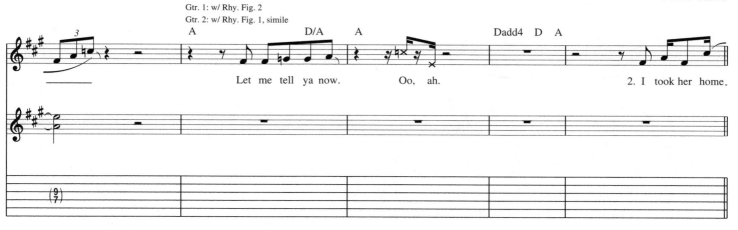

⊕ *Coda 1*

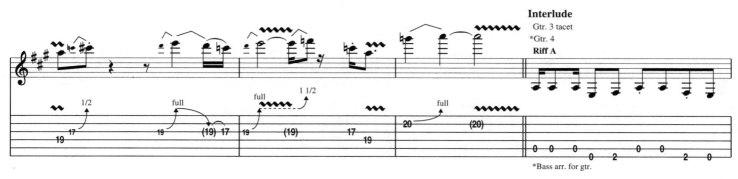

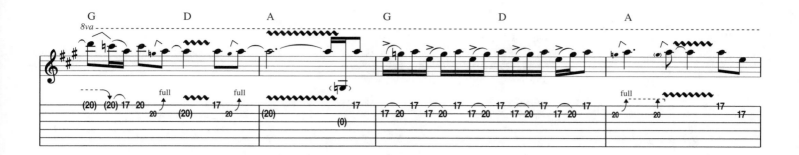

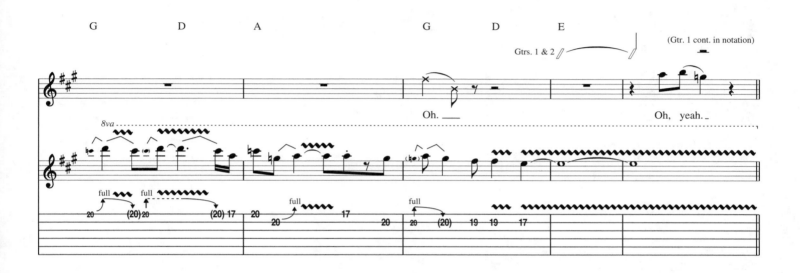

Bridge

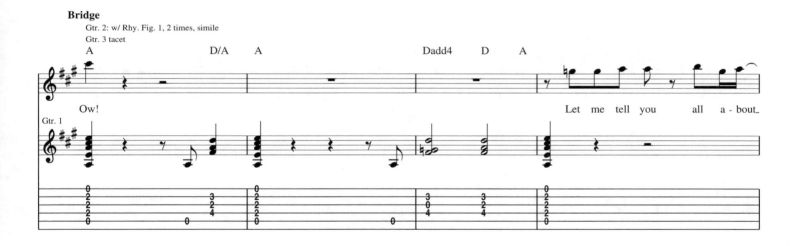

D.S. al Coda 2
(2nd lyrics)

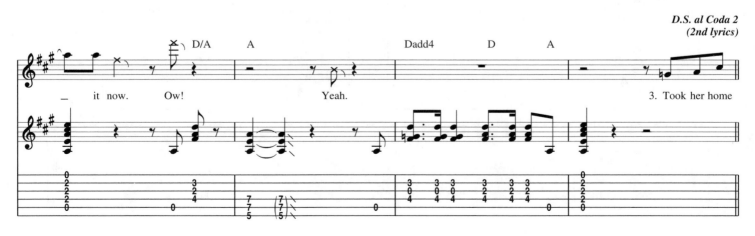

Back in Black

Words and Music by Angus Young, Malcolm Young and Brian Johnson

Guitar Solo

D.S. al Coda

Well, I'm

Gtr. 1

Gtr. 2

⊕ *Coda*

Interlude
w/Voc. ad lib.
N.C.(E5)

(A5)

(E5)

Well, I'm

Chorus
Gtrs. 1 & 2: w/Rhy. Fig. 2

A5   E5   B5   A5   B5   A5   E5   B5   A5   B5

back, _____ (I'm   back.   back. _____ Well, I'm
                                                                    I'm

G5   D   A5   G5   A5   G5   D   A5   G5   A5

back, _____   back, _____
back.   I'm   back.   I'm

E5   B5   A5   B5   A5   E5   B5   A5   B5   G5

back, _____   back. _____ It's back in black. ___ Yes, I'm
back.   I'm back.)

back in— black.—

I wan-na say it.

Outro/Guitar Solo

Badge

Words and Music by Eric Clapton and George Harrison

Guitar Solo

Gtr. 2: w/ Rhy. Fig. 2, 3 1/4 times, simile
Gtr. 1: w/ Rhy. Fig. 3, 3 1/4 times, simile

Born To Be Wild

Words and Music by Mars Bonfire

Pre-Chorus

Yeah, dar-lin' go make it hap - pen, __ take the world in a love em - brace.

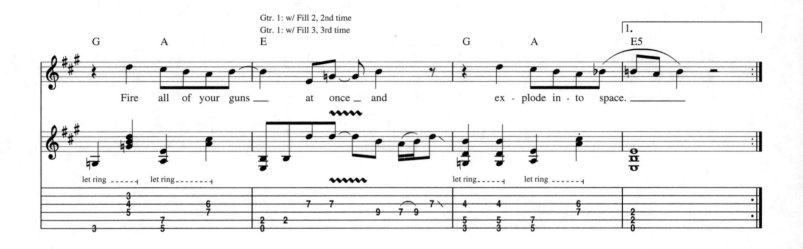

Fire all of your guns __ at once __ and ex - plode in - to space. __

Like a true na - ture's child __ we were born, born to be wild. __

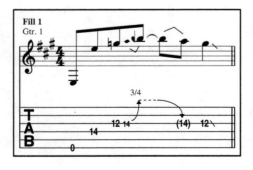

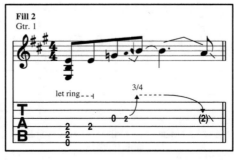

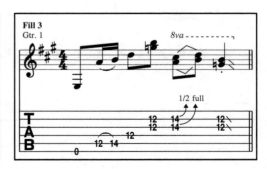

38

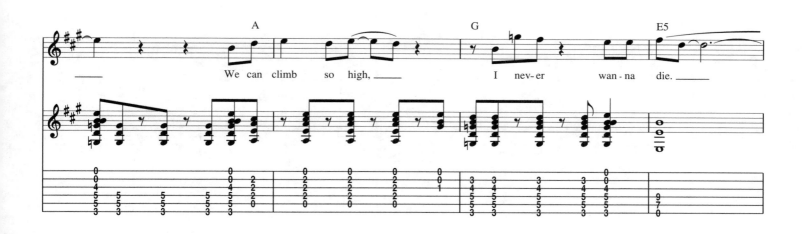

We can climb so high, _____ I nev-er wan-na die. _____

Chorus

Born to be wild. _____

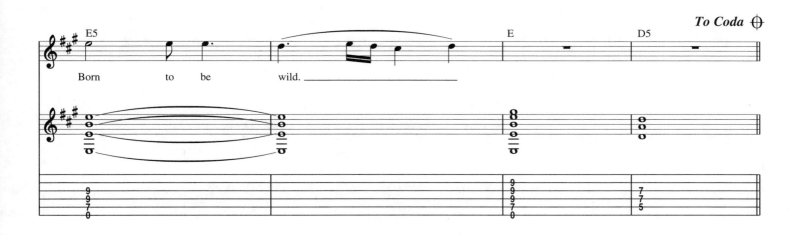

To Coda ⊕

Born to be wild. _____

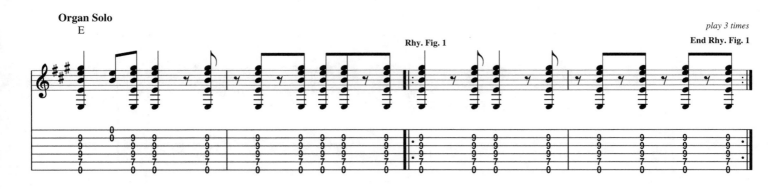

Organ Solo

play 3 times

Rhy. Fig. 1

End Rhy. Fig. 1

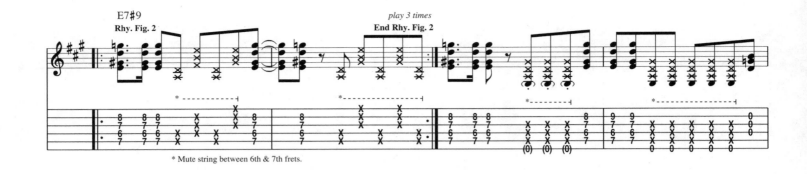

E7#9

Rhy. Fig. 2

play 3 times

End Rhy. Fig. 2

* Mute string between 6th & 7th frets.

D.S. al Coda

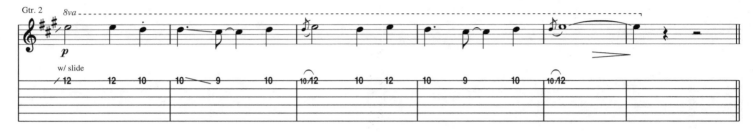

E
Gtr. 1

Gtrs. 1 & 2 tacet

Gtr. 2

8va

p

w/ slide

⊕ *Coda*

Outro

Gtr. 1: w/ Rhy. Fig 1, 4 times, simile

Gtr. 1: w/ Rhy. Fig. 2, 1 1/2 times

E

E7#9

8va

Gtr. 2

w/ slide

Fade Out

Gtr. 1: w/ Fill 4

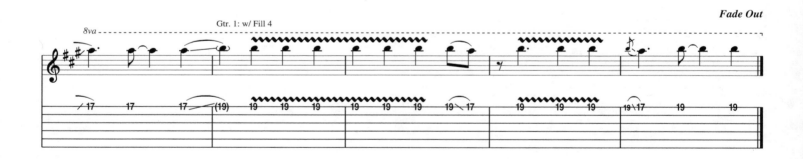

8va

Fill 4
Gtr. 1

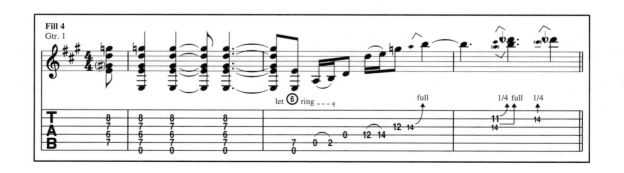

let ⑥ ring

full

1/4 full   1/4

40

Brown Eyed Girl

Words and Music by Van Morrison

Verse

Gtr. 2: w/ Rhy. Fig. 1, 4 times

3. So hard to find ___ my way now ___ that I'm all ___ on my ___ own. ___

I saw you just ___ the oth-er day; ___ my, ___ how you have grown. ___

Cast ___ my mem-'ry back ___ there, Lord. Some - times I'm o -

ver - come think - in' 'bout ___ it. Laugh - ing and a run - ning, hey, ___ hey, ___

Day Tripper

Words and Music by John Lennon and Paul McCartney

Got a good rea - son / for tak-ing the eas - y way out, __ now.
She's a big tea - ser. / She took me half __ the way there, _ now.
Tried to please _ her, / she on - ly played _ one night stands,. now.

She was a

Chorus

Gtr. 3: w/ Fill 1, 1st time
Gtr. 3: w/ Fill 2, 2nd time
Gtr. 3: w/ Fill 4, 3rd time (see p. 64)
Gtr. 3: w/ Fill 3, 2nd time

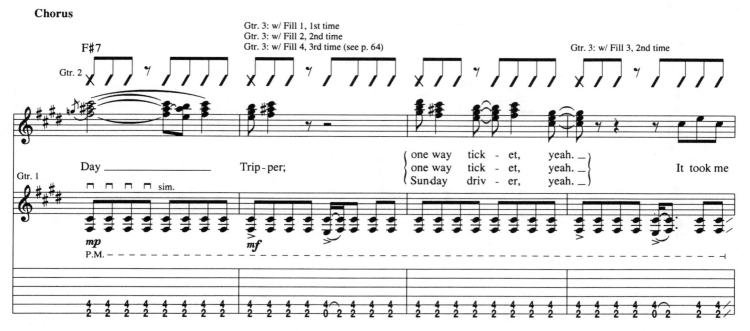

Day _____ Trip - per;
one way tick - et, yeah. __
one way tick - et, yeah. __
Sun-day driv - er, yeah. __

It took me

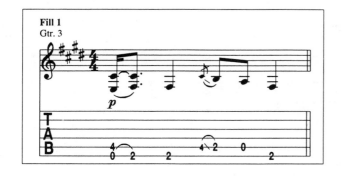

Fill 1
Gtr. 3

Fill 2
Gtr. 3

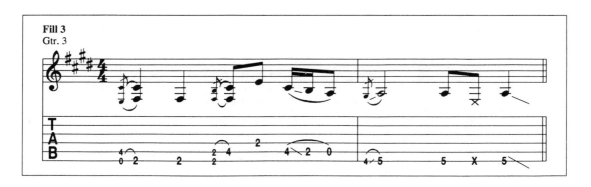

Fill 3
Gtr. 3

so _____ long   to find out, ___   and I found

out.

Interlude

Gtr. 3: w/ Riff A

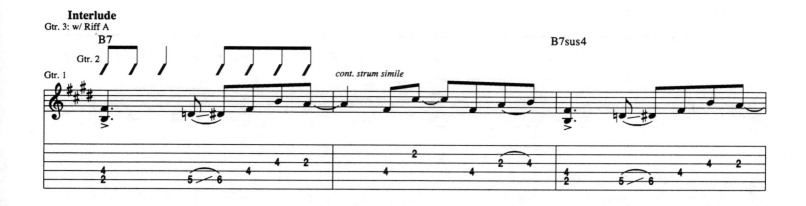

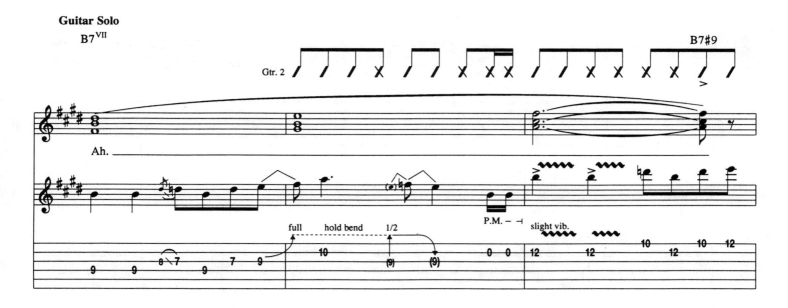

Guitar Solo

Gtr. 4: w/ Rhy. Fill 2

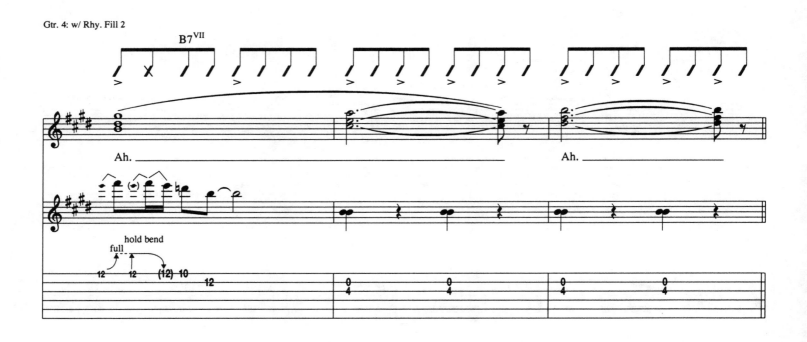

Ah. _____ Ah. _____

D.S. al Coda
(*take 1st ending*)

Breakdown

N.C. (E7)   Gtr. 2: w/ Rhy. Fig. 1

                               E   E7   E   E7   E E7

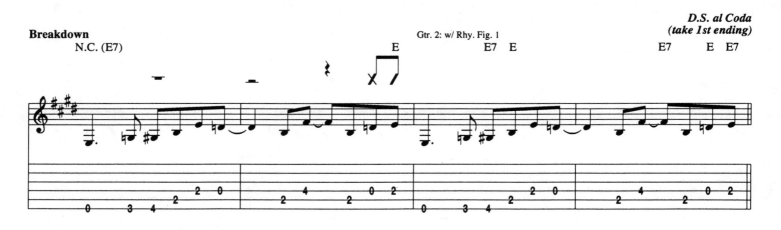

$\oplus$ *Coda*

Breakdown

Gtrs. 1 & 2

N.C. (E7)

Rhy. Fill 2
Gtr. 4 (overdub with Gtr. 1)

P.M. - - - - - - - ┐   P.M. - ┐   P.M. - ┐   P.M. - ┐   P.M. - ┐

Gtr. 2: w/ Rhy. Fig. 1, 2 times

Out-Chorus
Gtr. 2: w/ Rhy. Fig. 1, till fade

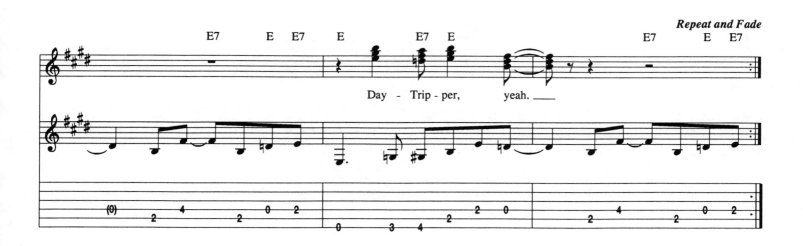

Day - Trip - per,

Repeat and Fade

Day - Trip - per,   yeah. ___

Fill 4
Gtr. 3

Don't Fear the Reaper

Words and Music by Donald Roeser

-er. Ba-by take my hand. _ Don't fear the reap - er. We'll be a - ble to fly. _ Don't fear the reap -

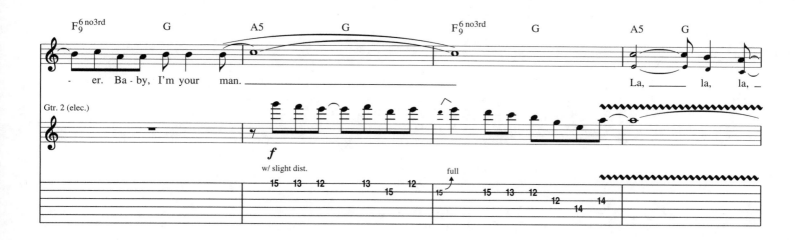

-er. Ba-by, I'm your man. _____ La, _____ la, la, _

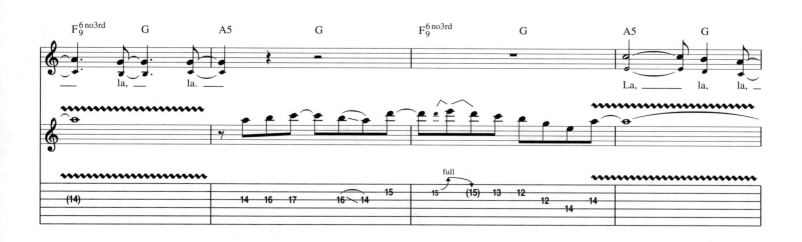

— la, _ la. _ La, _____ la, la, _

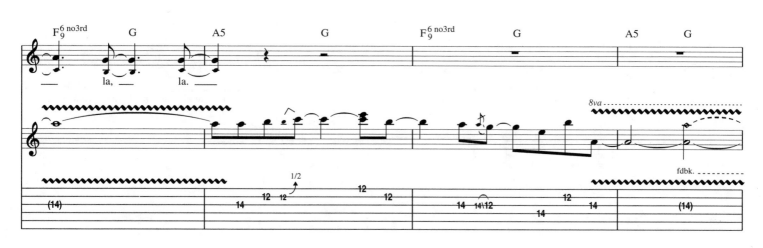

— la, _ la.

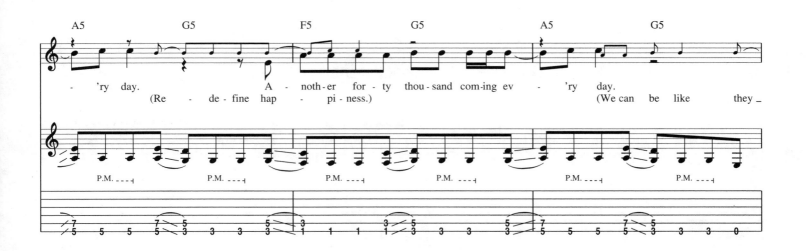

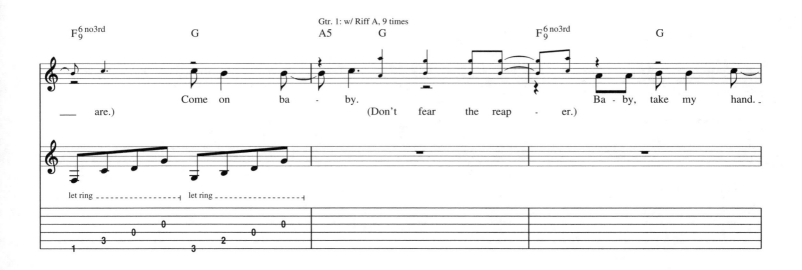

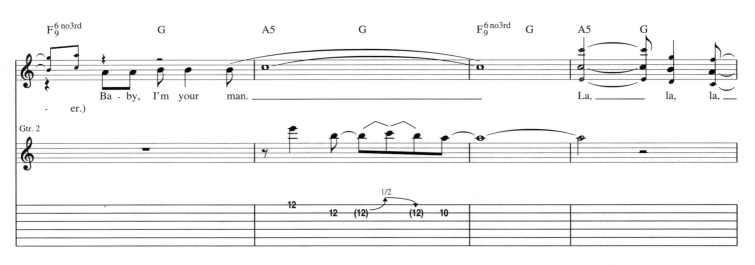

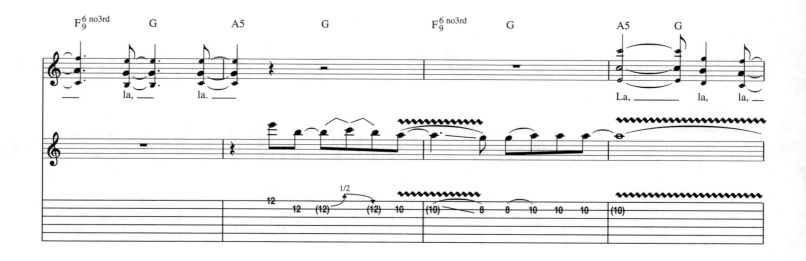

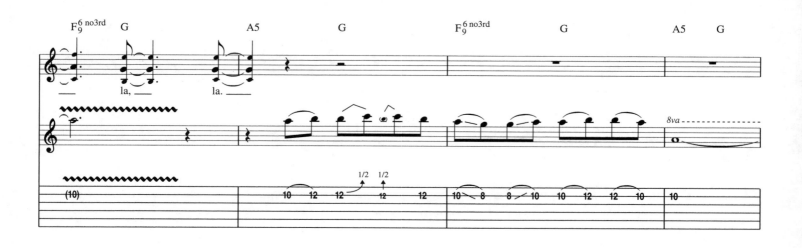

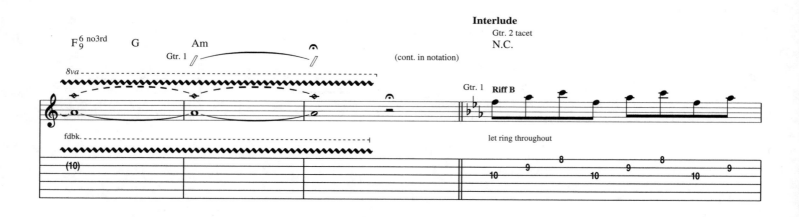

Guitar Solo

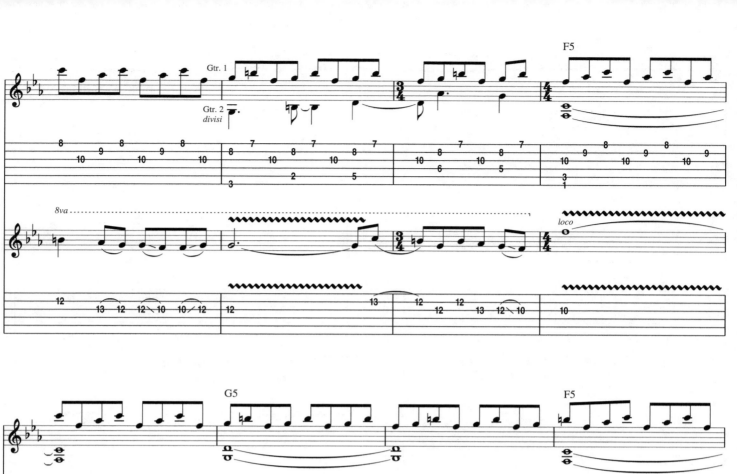

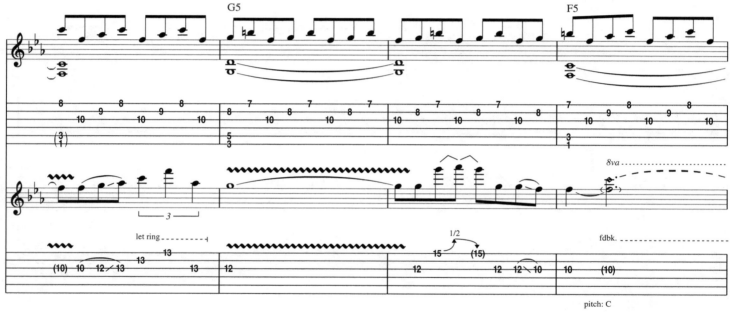

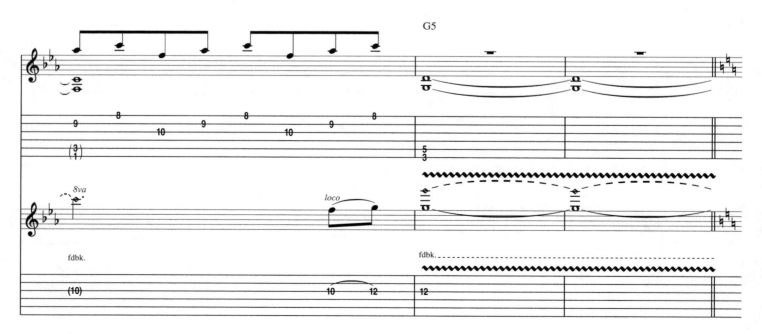

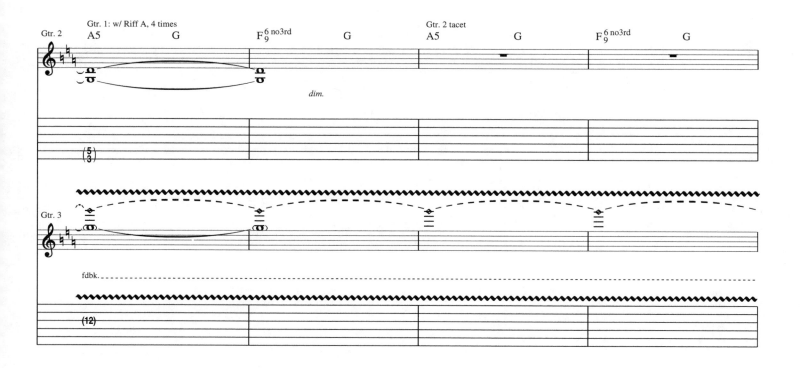

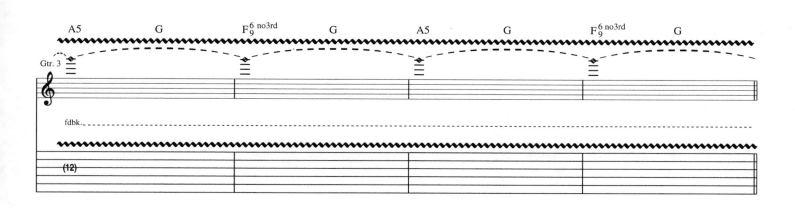

Verse

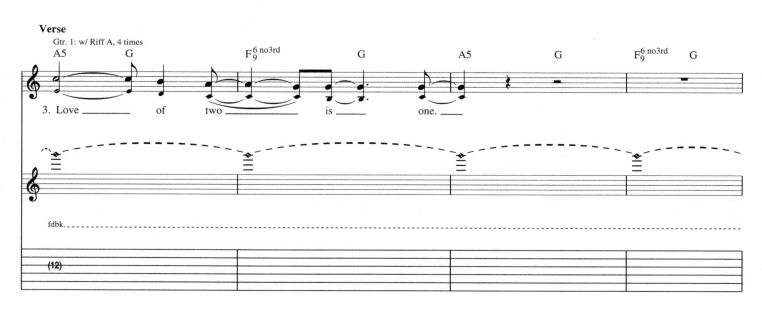

3. Love _____ of two _____ is _____ one. _____

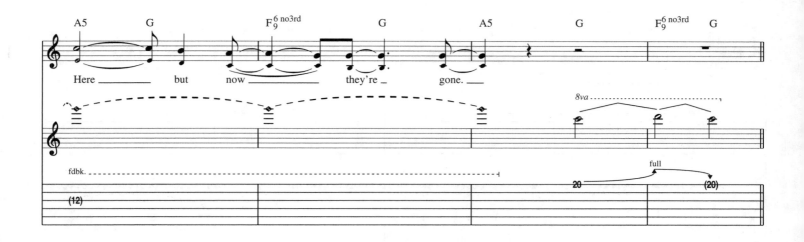

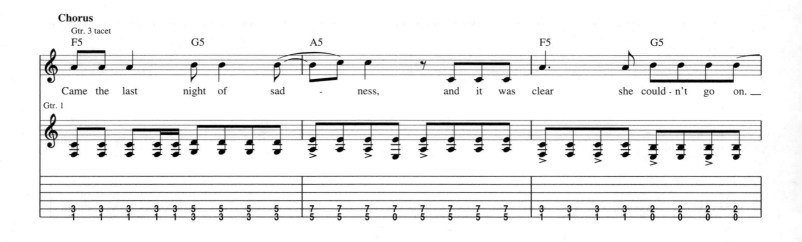

Chorus

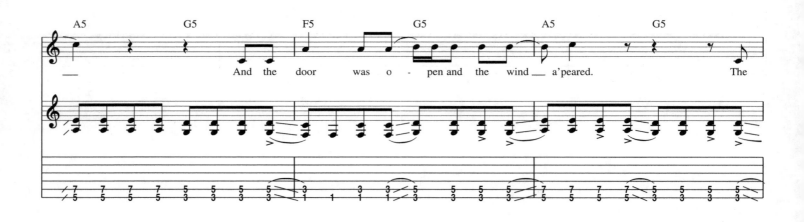

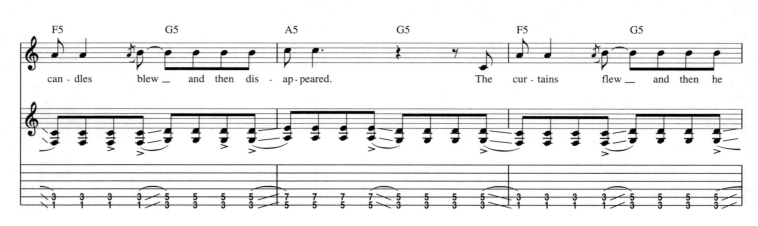

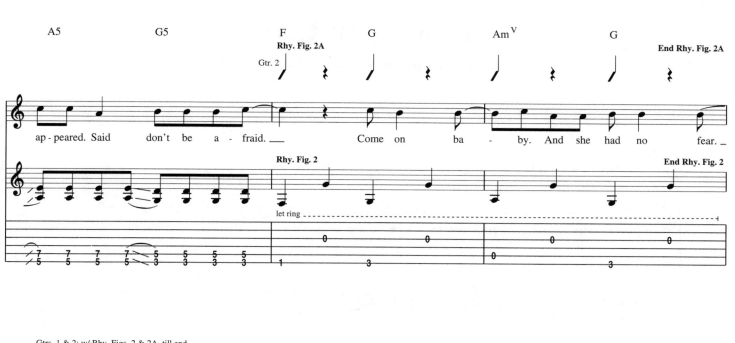

ap - peared. Said   don't be a - fraid. ___   Come on   ba - by. And she had   no   fear. ___

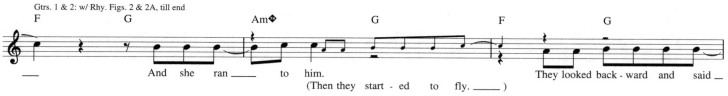

Gtrs. 1 & 2: w/ Rhy. Figs. 2 & 2A, till end

___   And she ran ___ to him.
(Then they start - ed   to   fly. ___)
They looked back - ward and said ___

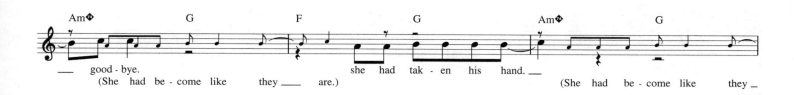

___   good - bye.
(She had be - come like   they ___ are.)
she had tak - en his hand. ___
(She had be - come like   they ___

___   are.)
Come   on   ba - by.
(Don't   fear   the   reap - er.)

*Two gtrs. arr. for one.

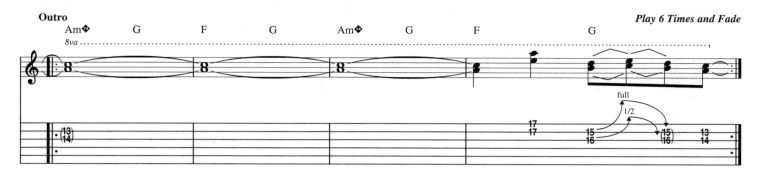

Outro
Play 6 Times and Fade

Am◆   G   F   G   Am◆   G   F   G

63

Drive My Car

Words and Music by John Lennon and Paul McCartney

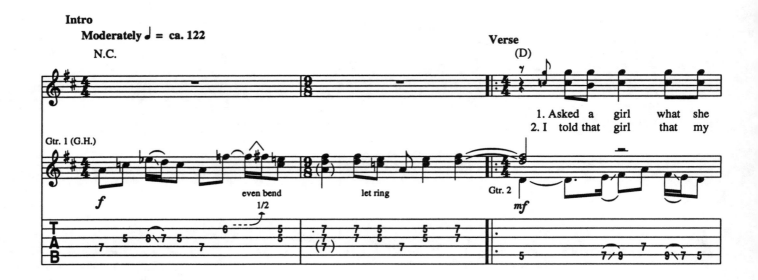

Guitar Solo
(P.McC.)

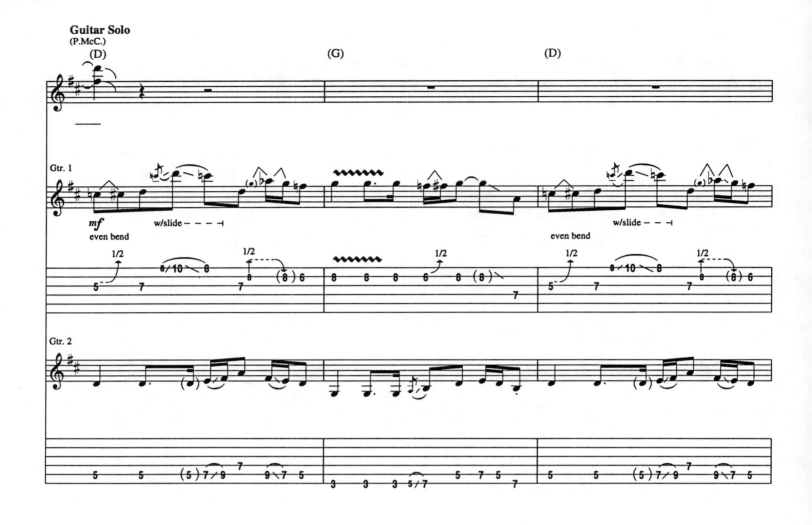

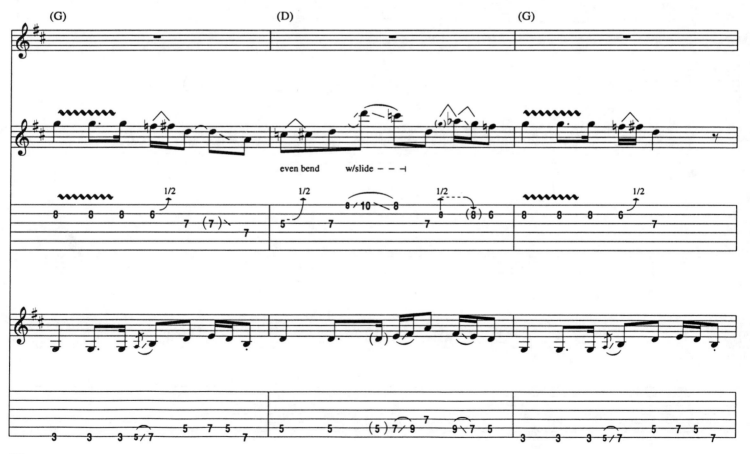

%. Chorus

(Am7)

(Bm)

"Ba - by, you can drive my   car.__

w/slide

(G)   (Bm)   (G)

Yes, I'm gon - na   be   a   star.__

Gtr. 1 tacet
Gtr. 2

(Bm)   (E)   (A)   (D)   (G)

To Coda ⊕

Ba - by, you can drive my   car,__   and may - be I'll love __ you."

Verse

3. I told that girl I could start right a - way, ____

and she said, "Lis-ten babe, __ I got some-thin' to say. ____ I got no car an' it's

break-in' my heart, __ but I found a driv - er, and that's a start. __

D.S. al Coda

Coda

Beep, beep, mm - beep, beep, yeah! ____

Gimme Three Steps

Words and Music by Allen Collins and Ronnie Van Zant

* Gtr. 3 is doubled throughout.

there fel-low with the hair col-ored yel - low,
wait a min-ute mis-ter I did - n't ev - en kiss her,
and screamed at Lin-da Lu and that's the

what you try-in' to prove?
don't want no trou-ble with you.
break I was look-in' for.

'Cause that's
And I know
And you could

my wo-man there and I'm a man who cares and this might be all for you."
you don't owe me but I wish you would let me ask one fa - vor from you.
hear me scream-in' a mile a - way as I was head-in' out t'wards the door.

Guitar Solo

I said, "Ex - cuse me!"

Gtr. 3

pick w/fingers

Rhy. Fill 2
Gtr. 2

Rhy. Fill 4
Gtrs. 1 & 2

For sure!

* implied tonality

Coda

Outro Guitar Solo

Gts. 1 & 2: w/ Rhy. Fig. 1, 2 times

Gtr. 3

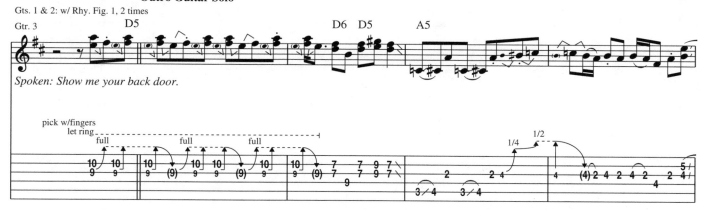

Spoken: Show me your back door.

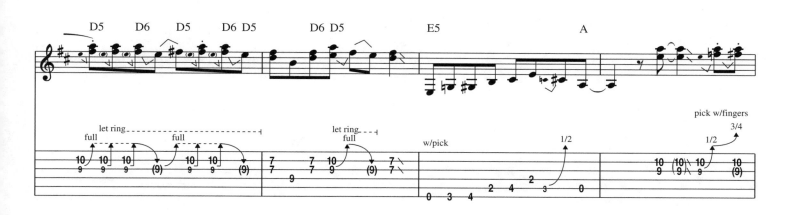

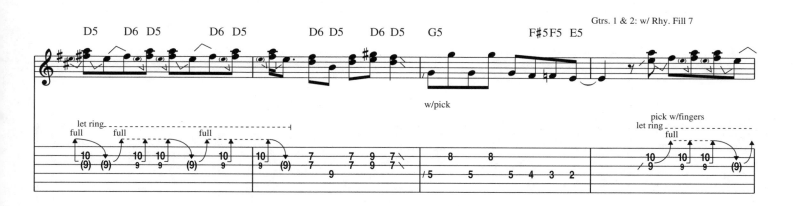

Gtrs. 1 & 2: w/ Rhy. Fill 7

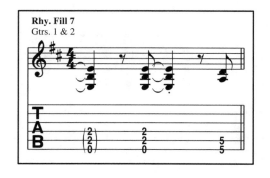

Rhy. Fill 7
Gtrs. 1 & 2

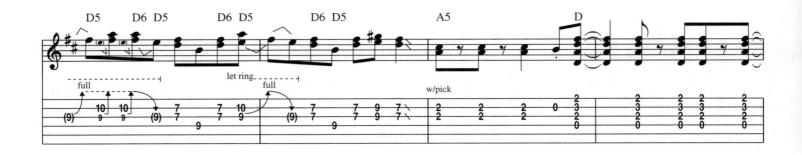

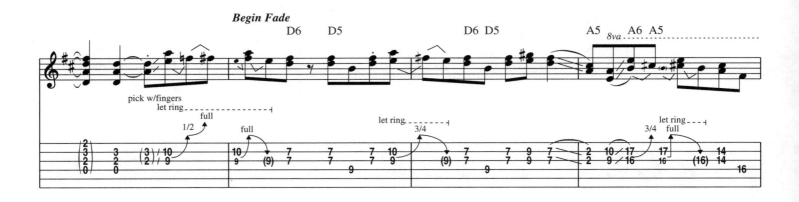

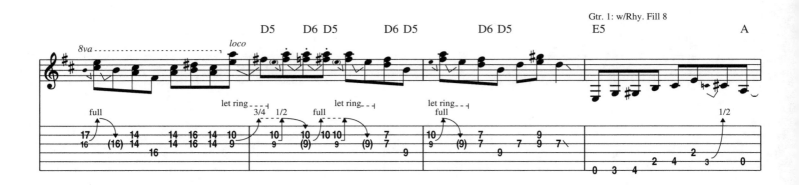

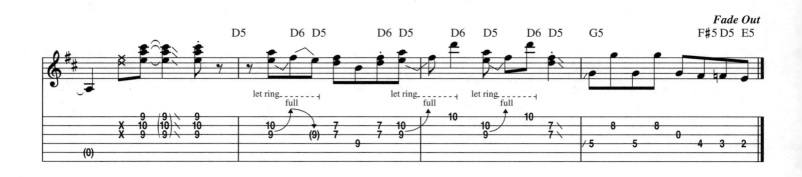

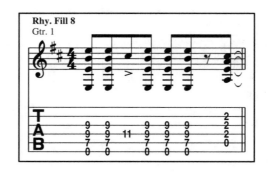

Gloria

Words and Music by Van Morrison

Hello, I Love You
(Won't You Tell Me Your Name?)

Words and Music by The Doors

* Key signature denotes A Mixolydian.
** Chord symbols reflect overall tonality.

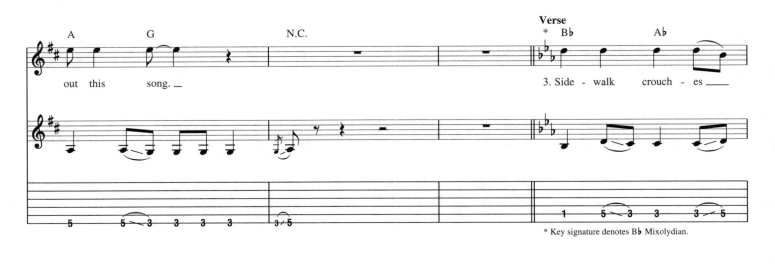

out   this   song. ___

3. Side - walk   crouch - es ___

* Key signature denotes B♭ Mixolydian.

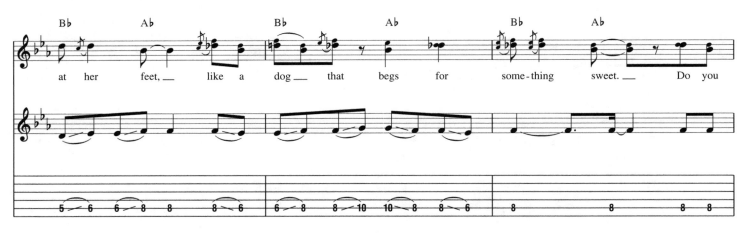

at   her   feet, ___   like a   dog ___   that   begs   for   some-thing   sweet. ___   Do   you

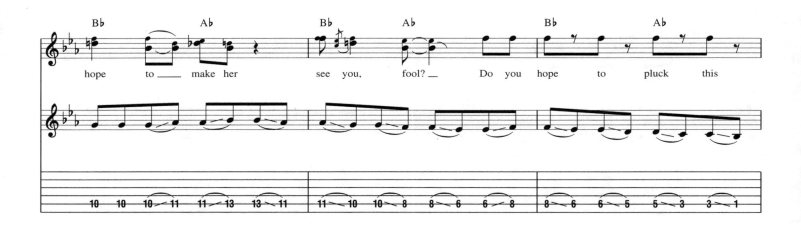

hope   to ___   make her   see   you,   fool? ___   Do   you   hope   to   pluck   this

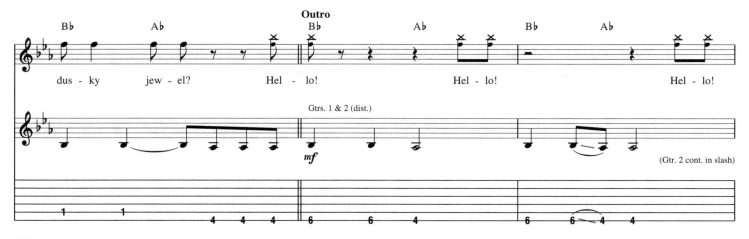

dus - ky   jew - el?   Hel - lo!   Hel - lo!   Hel - lo!

Gtrs. 1 & 2 (dist.)

mf

(Gtr. 2 cont. in slash)

84

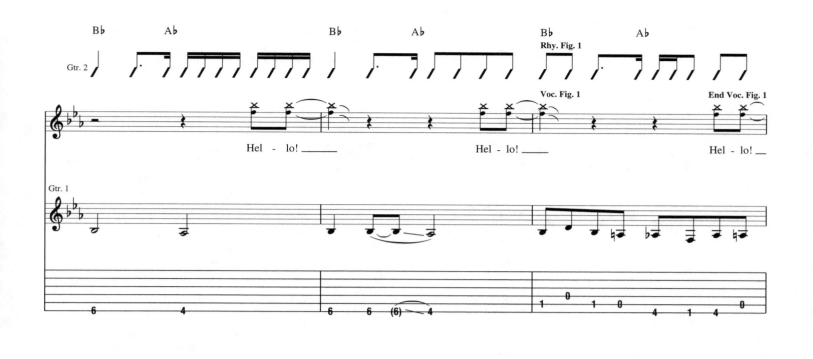

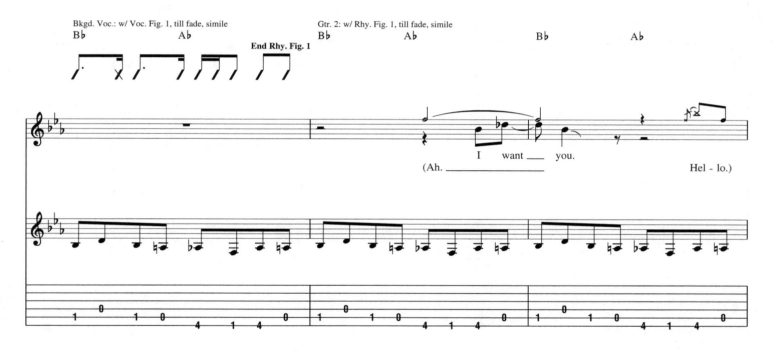

Hey Joe

Words and Music by Billy Roberts

I said, where you go-in' with that gun in your hand? Al - right.

Ooh. I'm go-in' down to shoot my old la - dy,

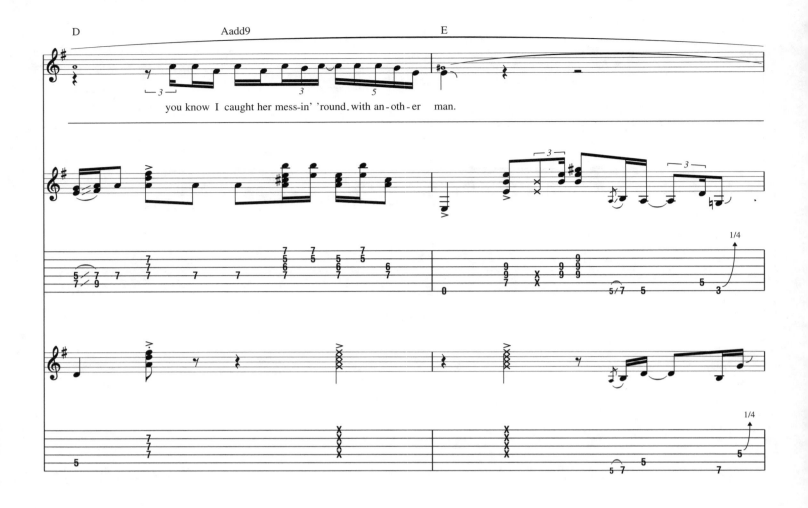

you know I caught her mess-in' 'round with an-oth-er man.

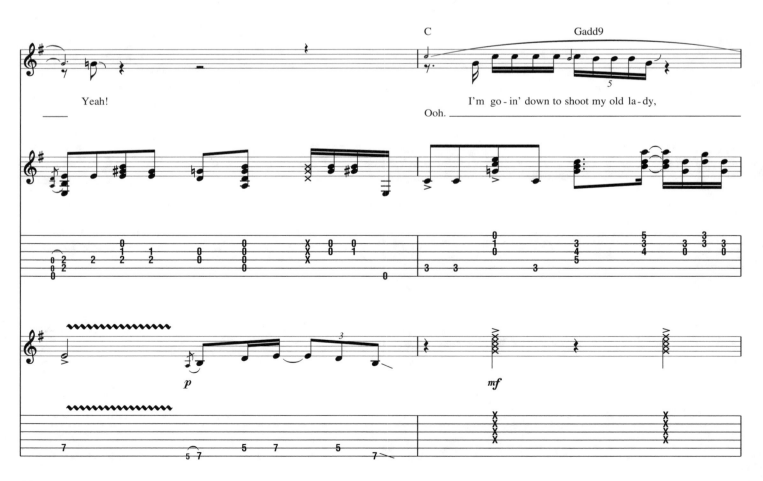

Yeah!

Ooh.

I'm go-in' down to shoot my old la-dy,

p

mf

you know I caught her mess-in' 'round with an - oth-er man. _ Huh! And that ain't

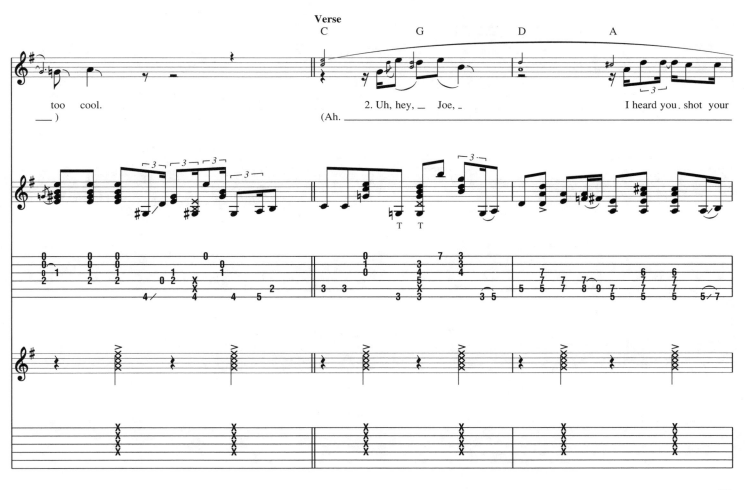

too cool.

—)

Verse

(Ah. _

2. Uh, hey, _ Joe, _ I heard you. shot your

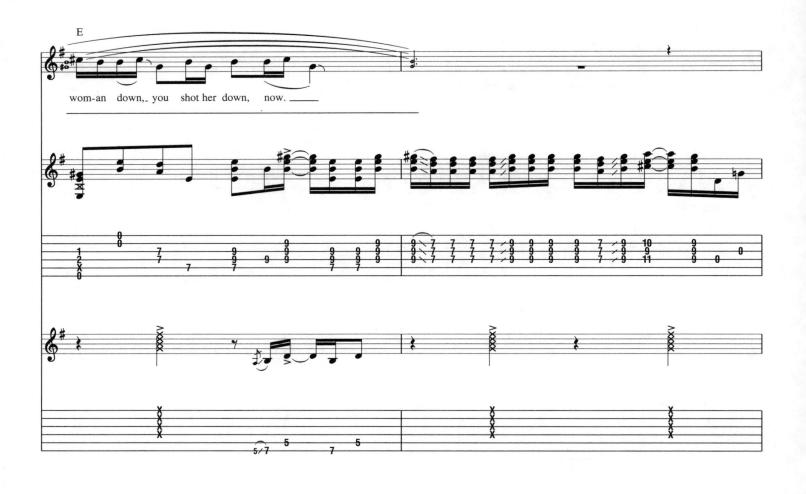

wom-an down,_ you shot her down, now. _____

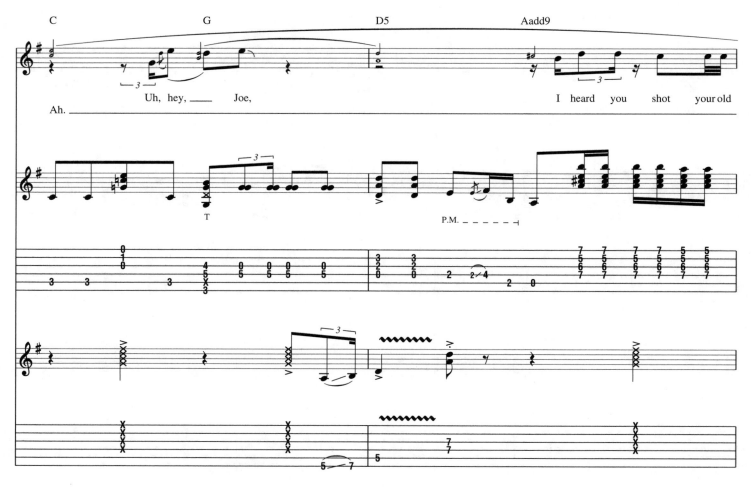

C   G   D5   Aadd9

Ah. _____   Uh, hey, _____ Joe,   I heard you shot your old

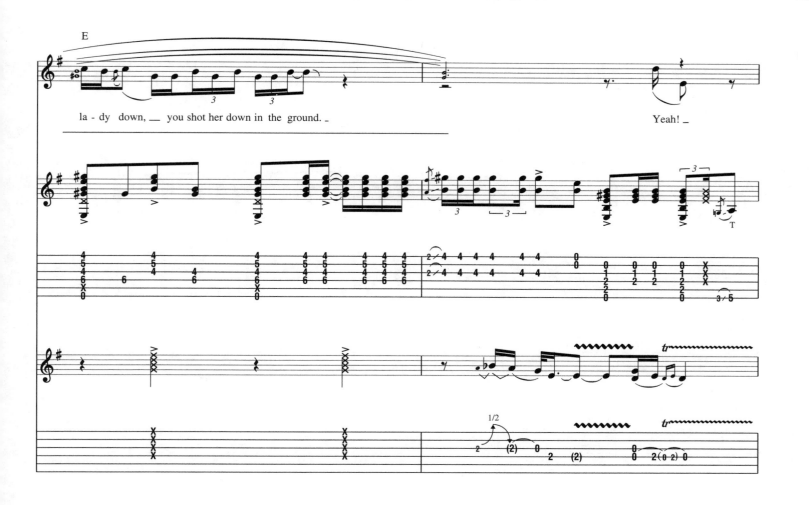

la - dy down, __ you shot her down in the ground. __ Yeah! __

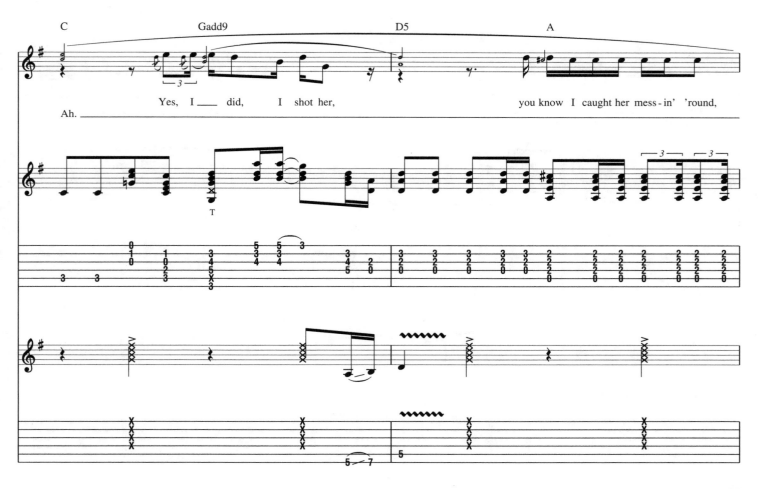

Yes, I __ did, I shot her, you know I caught her mess - in' 'round,
Ah. _____

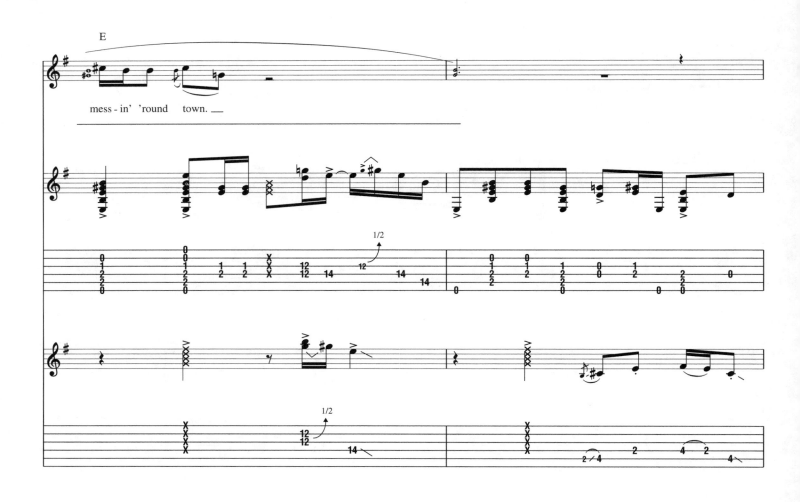

mess - in' 'round   town. ___

Uh, yes I did, I   shot her,   you know I   caught my old la - dy mess-in' 'round

Ah. _____

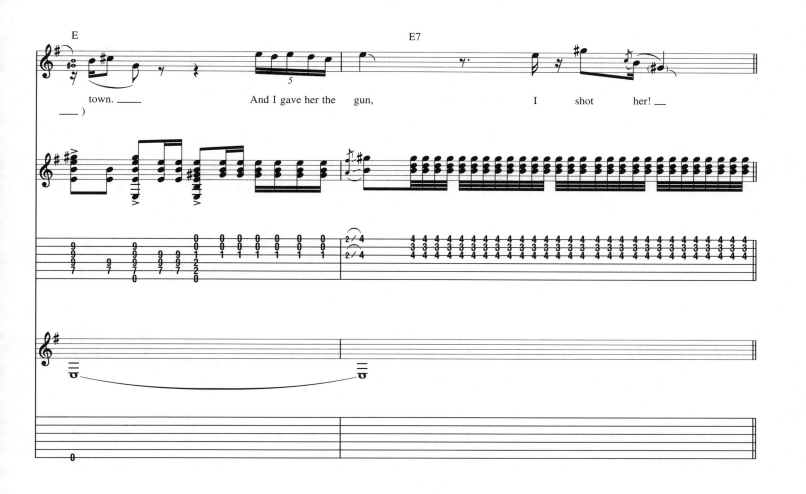

town. _____   And I gave her the gun,   I shot her! _____
_____)

Guitar Solo

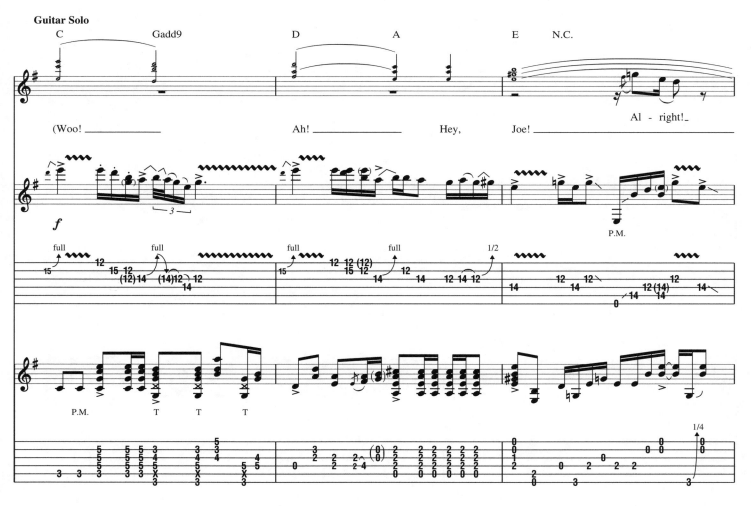

(Woo! _____   Ah! _____   Hey,   Joe! _____   Al - right!_

93

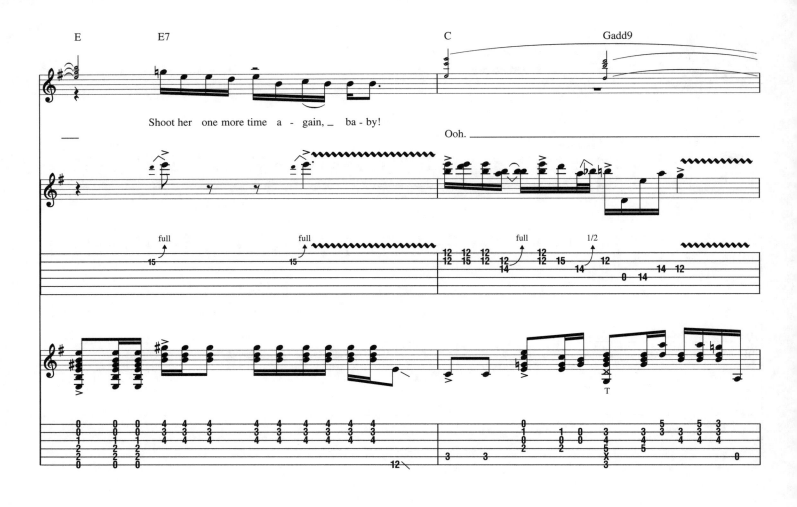

Shoot her one more time a - gain, _ ba - by!

Ooh. _____

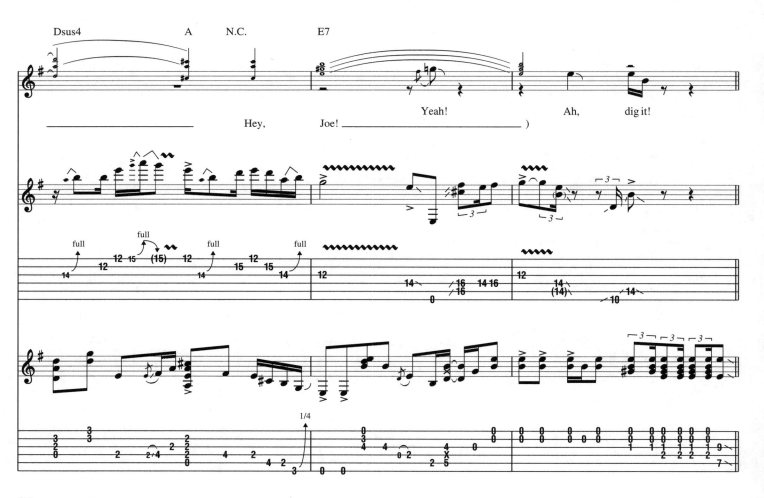

Hey, Joe! _____ Yeah! Ah, dig it!

Interlude

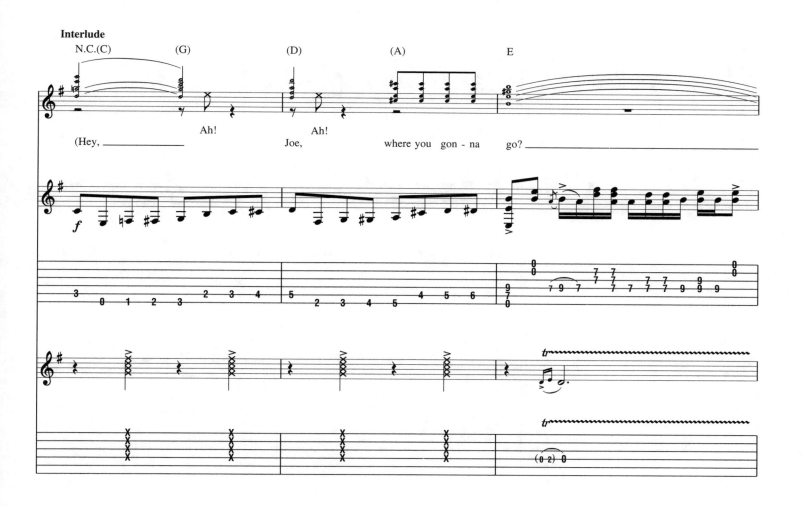

Ah!   Ah!

(Hey, _____ Joe,   where you gon-na go? _____

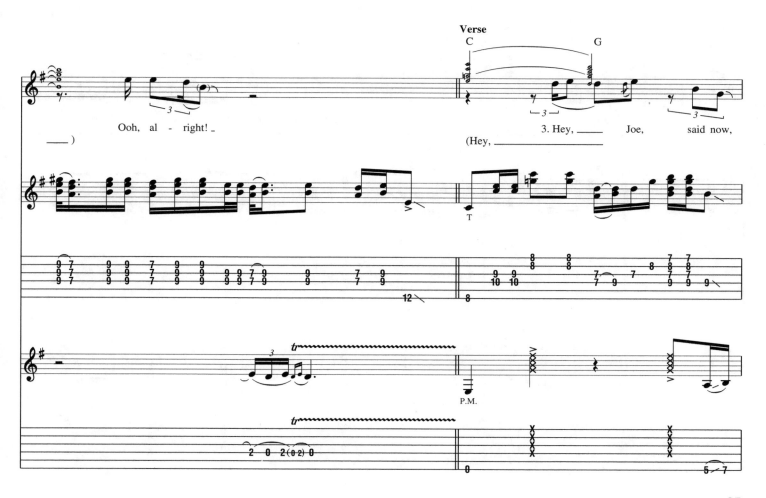

Ooh, al - right! _

_____)

3. Hey, _____ Joe,   said now,

(Hey, _____

Verse

uh, where you gon-na run to now, _ where you gon-na run to? ___

Joe, where you gon-na go?_____

Yeah.

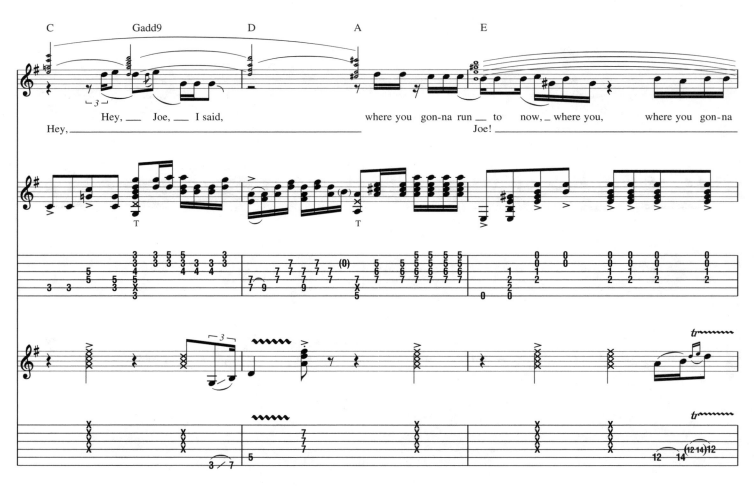

Hey, ___ Joe, ___ I said,

Hey,_____

where you gon-na run _ to now, _ where you,

Joe!

where you gon-na

go? ___   Well, dig it!   I'm go-in' way down   south, __   way down __ to

Hey, _____

Mex-i - co __ way! __   Al - right! __   I'm go-in' way down   south, __

Joe! _____   Hey, _____

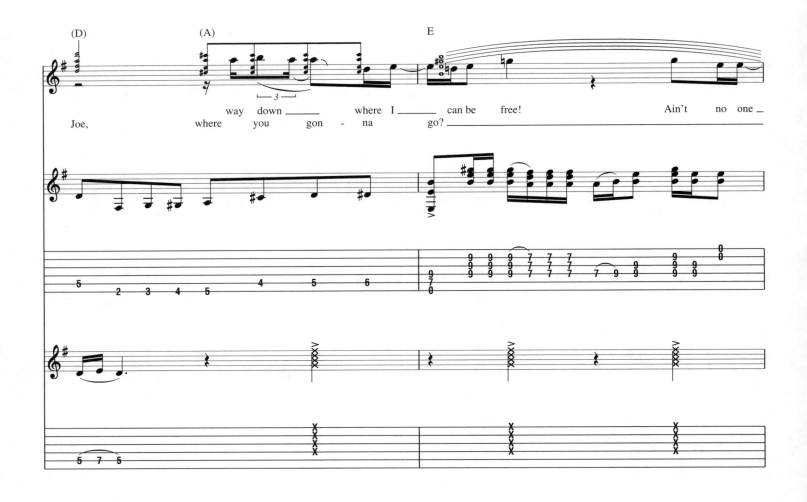

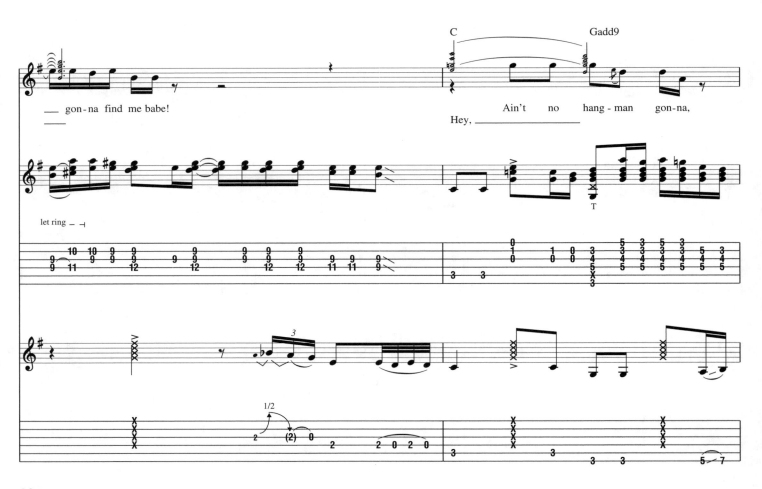

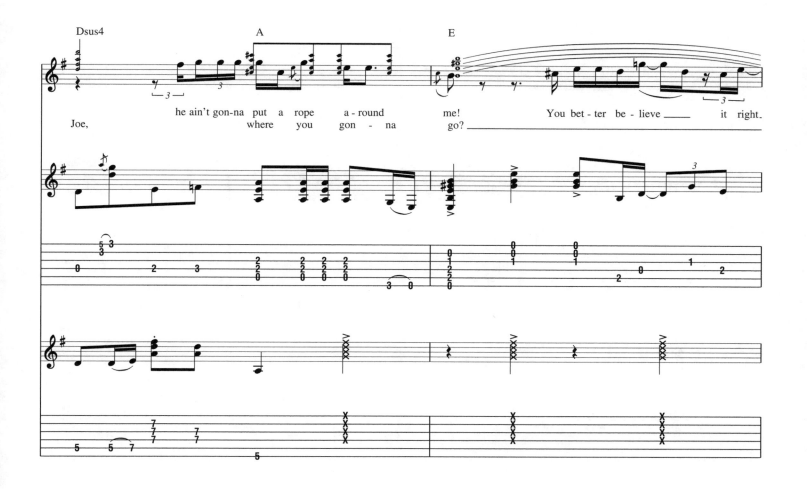

he ain't gon-na put a rope a - round me!

Joe, where you gon - na go?

You bet - ter be - lieve ___ it right.

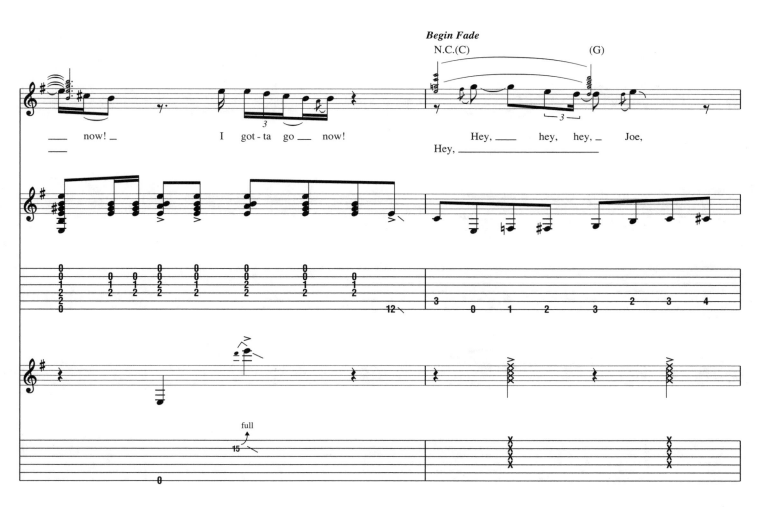

Begin Fade

N.C.(C)   (G)

___ now! ___   I got - ta go ___ now!   Hey, ___ hey, hey, ___ Joe,

Hey, _____

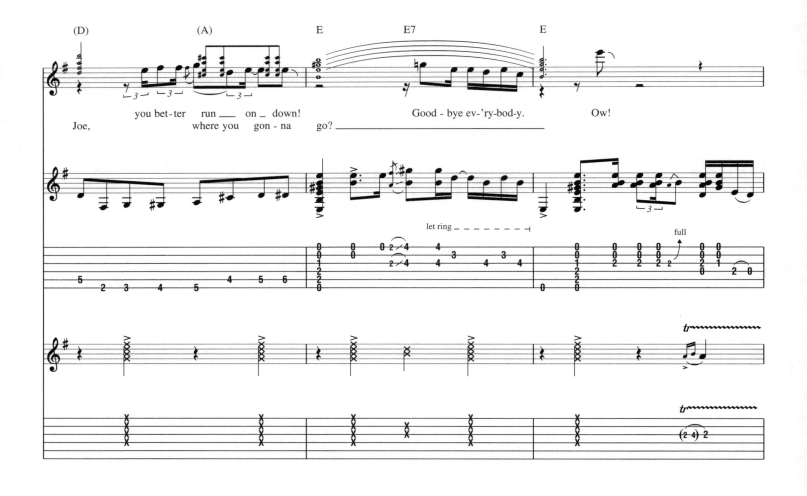

you bet-ter run ___ on ___ down!   Good - bye ev-'ry-bod-y.   Ow!

Joe,   where you gon - na   go? _____

Fade Out

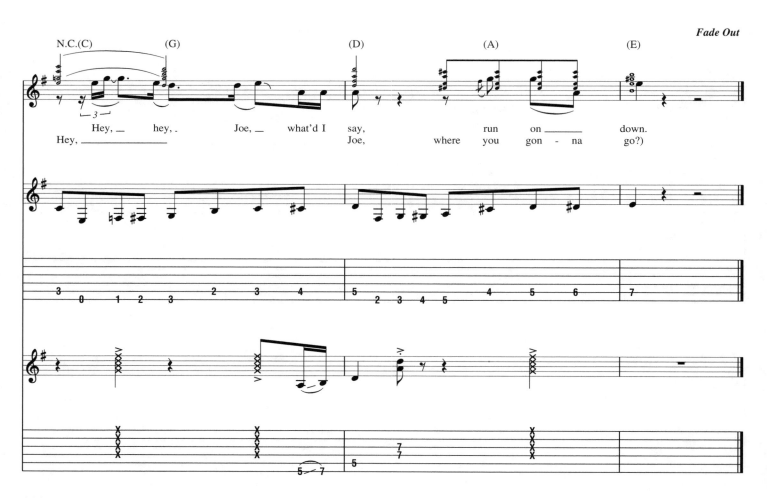

Hey, ___ hey, . ___ Joe, ___ what'd I   say,   run   on _____ down.

Hey, _____   Joe,   where you gon - na   go?)

Jailbreak

Words and Music by Philip Parris Lynott

Jailhouse Rock

Words and Music by Jerry Leiber and Mike Stoller

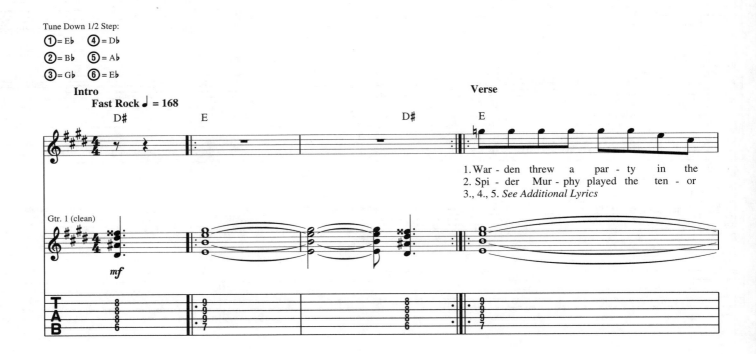

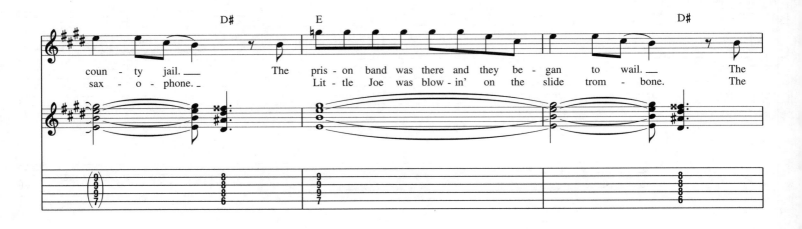

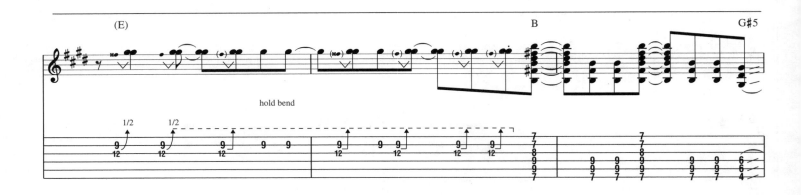

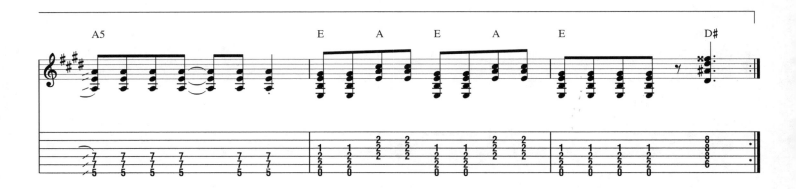

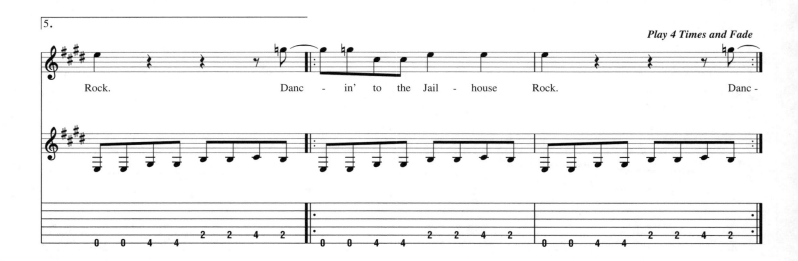

Additional Lyrics

3. Number forty-seven said to number three,
   "You the cutest jailbird I ever did see.
   I sure would be delighted with your company.
   Come on, and do the Jailhouse Rock with me."

4. Sad Sack was sittin' on a block of stone,
   Way over in the corner weepin' all alone.
   The warden said, "Hey, buddy, don't you be no square.
   If you can't find a partner use a wooden chair."

5. Shifty Henry said to Bugs "For heaven's sake,
   No one's lookin', now's our chance to make a break."
   Bugs, he turned to Shifty and he said, "Nix, nix,
   I wanna stick around awhile to get my kicks."

Message in a Bottle

Written and Composed by Sting

Pre-Chorus

Gtr. 3 tacet

Gtr. 3: w/ Fill 3, 3rd time

I'll send _ an S. ___ O. _ S. _ to the world. I'll send _ an S. ___ O. _ S. _ to the world.

Gtr. 3: w/ Fill 1, 2nd time

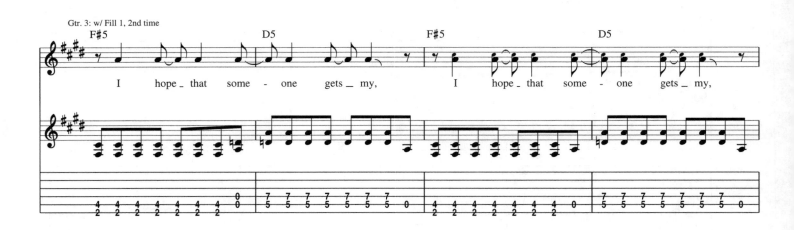

I hope _ that some - one gets _ my, I hope _ that some - one gets _ my,

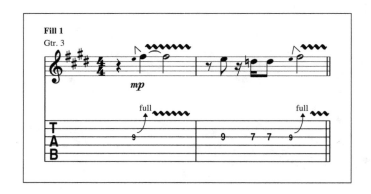

Fill 1

Gtr. 3

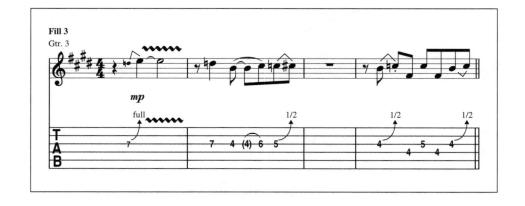

Fill 3

Gtr. 3

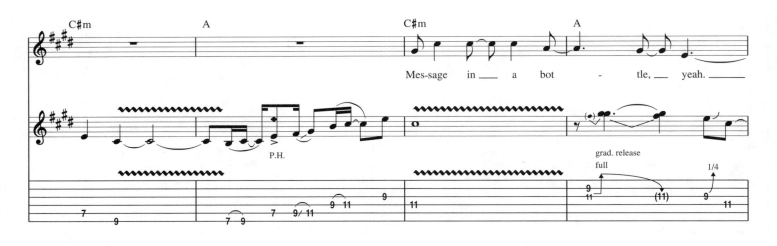

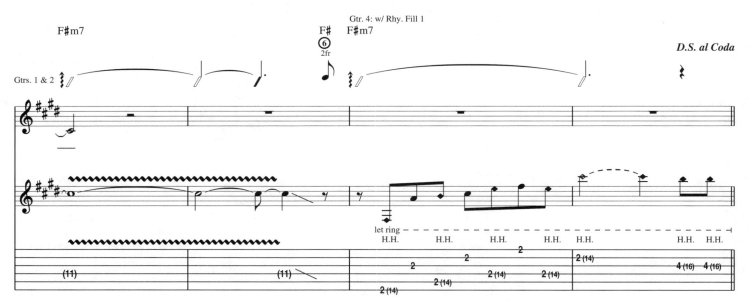

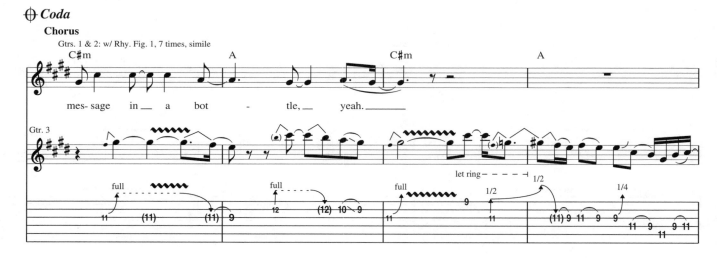

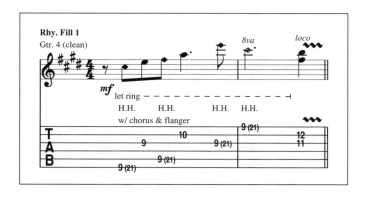

Additional Lyrics

Woke up this morning,
I don't believe what I saw.
Hundred billion bottles washed up on the shore.
Seems I never noticed being alone.
Hundred billion castaways,
Looking for a home.

Mississippi Queen

Words and Music by Leslie West, Felix Pappalardi, Corky Laing and David Rea

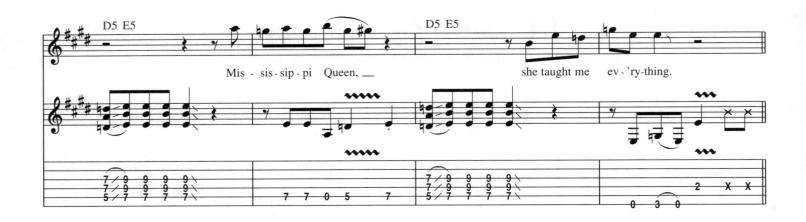

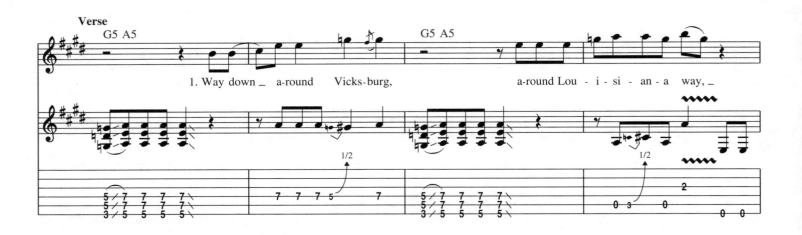

Verse

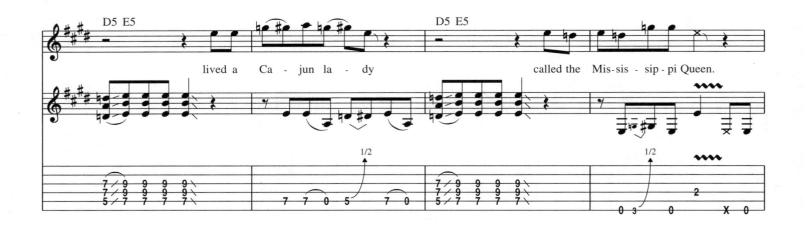

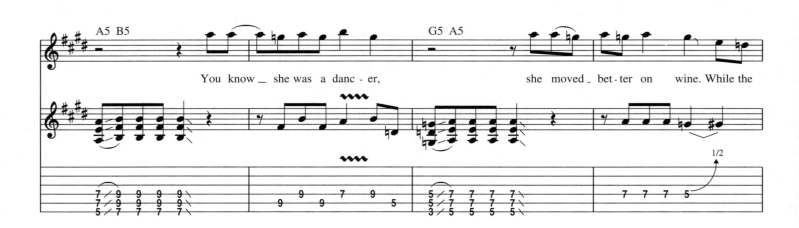

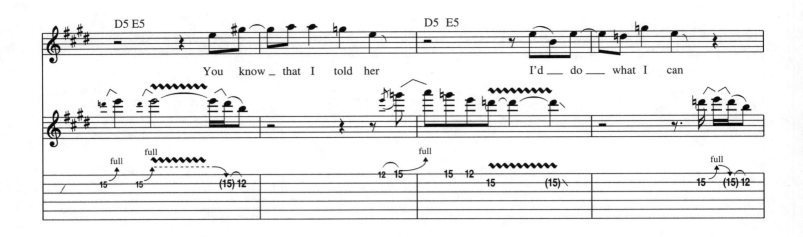
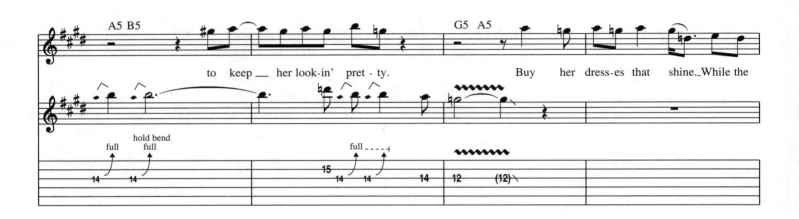
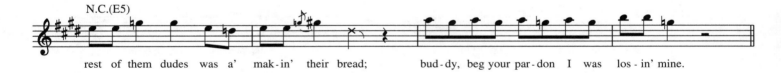
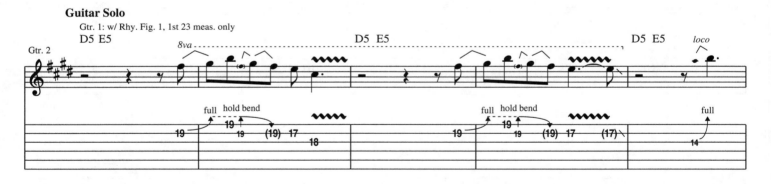
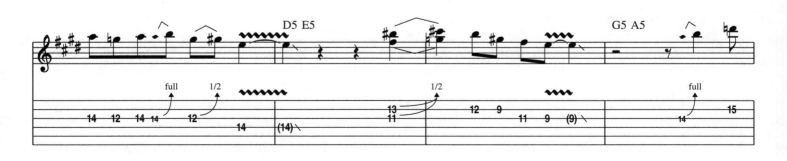

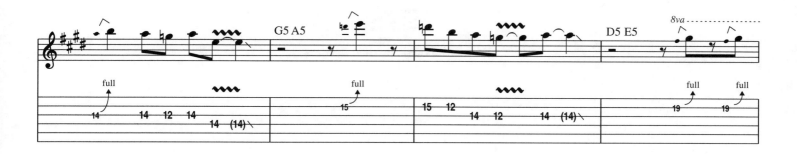

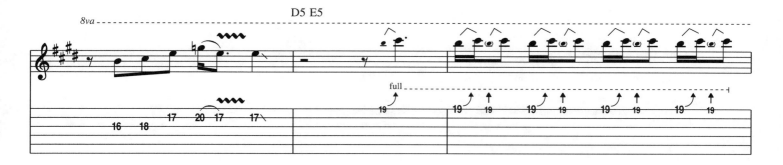

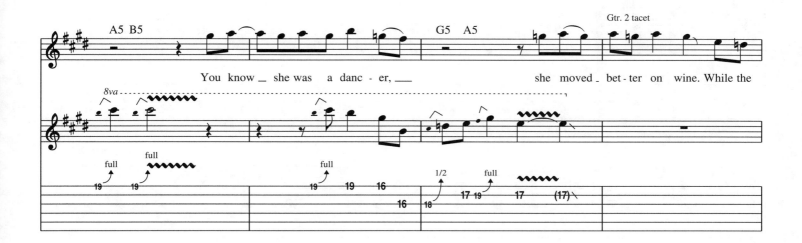

You know __ she was __ a danc - er, ___ she moved _ bet - ter on wine. While the

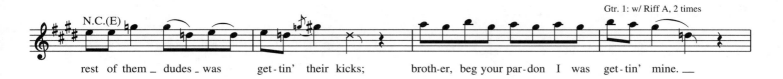

rest of them _ dudes _ was get - tin' their kicks; broth - er, beg your par - don I was get - tin' mine. __

Hey, _____ Mis - sis - sip - pi Queen. __

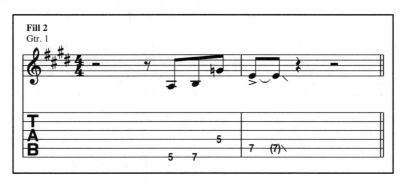

1979

Words and Music by Billy Corgan

121

No Particular Place to Go

Words and Music by Chuck Berry

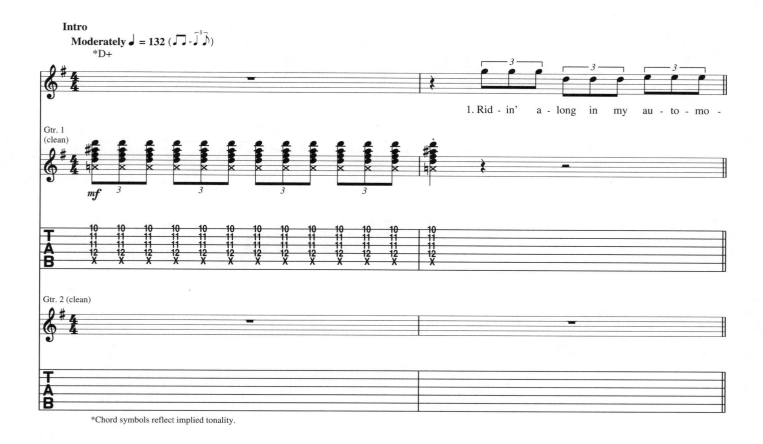

*Chord symbols reflect implied tonality.

I stole a kiss at the turn of a mile.
The night was young and the moon _ was gold,

My cu - ri - os - i - ty run - nin' wild. _
so we both de - cid - ed to take a stroll. _

Cruis - in' and play - in' the ra - di - o
Can you i - mag - ine the way _ I felt?

with no par - tic - u - lar place to go
I could - n't un - fas - ten her safe - ty belt.

2. Rid - in' a - long in my au - to - mo -
4. Rid - in' a - long in my cal - a - boose, _

End Rhy. Fig. 1

Verse

Gtr. 2: w/ Rhy. Fig. 1

bile,
I's anx - ious to tell her the way I feel.
still try - in' to get __ her belt a - loose.

Gtr. 1

So I told her soft - ly and sin - cere,
All __ the way home I held a grudge

and she leaned and whis - pered in my
for the safe - ty belt that would - n't budge. _

Cud - dl - in' more and driv - in' slow
Cruis - in' and play - in' the ra - di - o

To Coda ✛

with no par - tic - u - lar place to go.
with no par - tic - u - lar place to

Guitar Solo

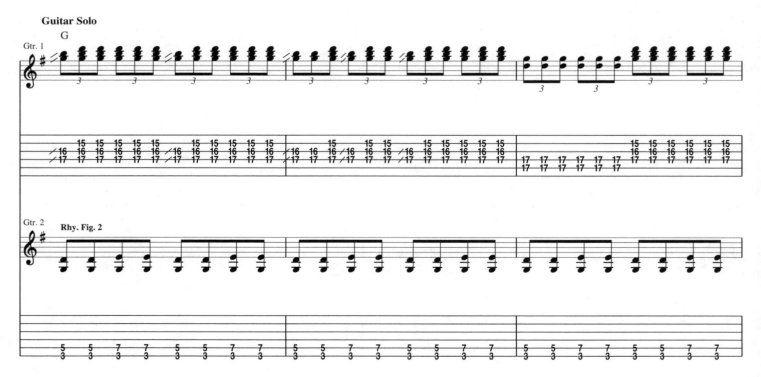

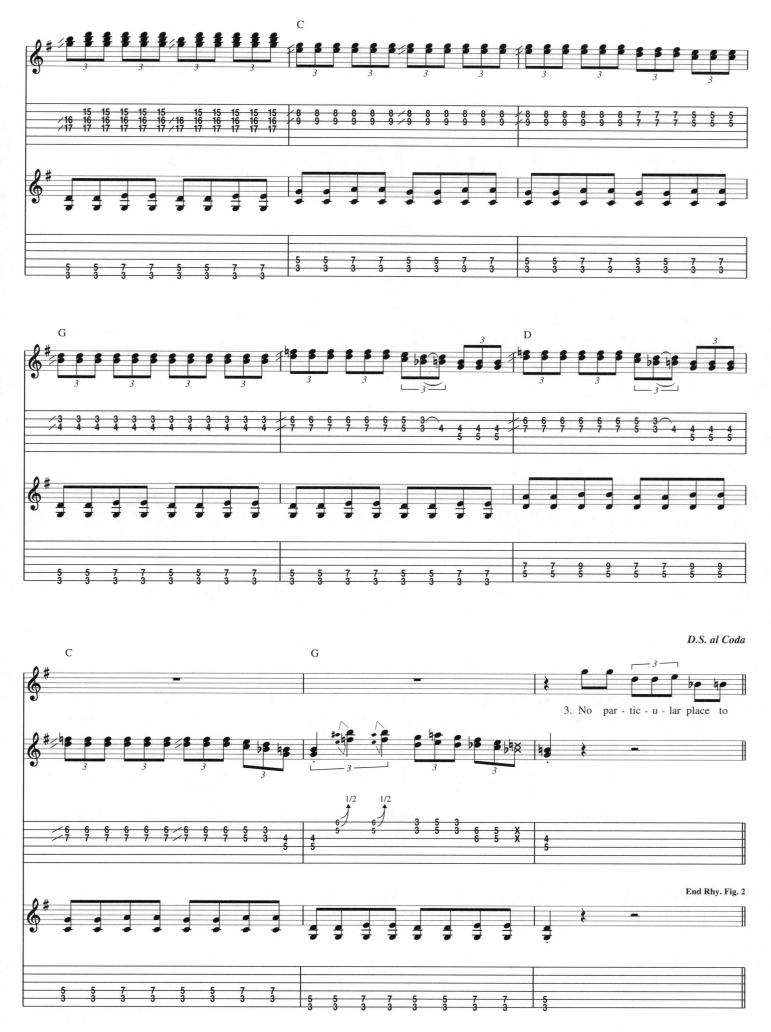

3. No par - tic - u - lar place to

Coda

Outro-Guitar Solo
Gtr. 2 w/ Rhy. Fig. 2

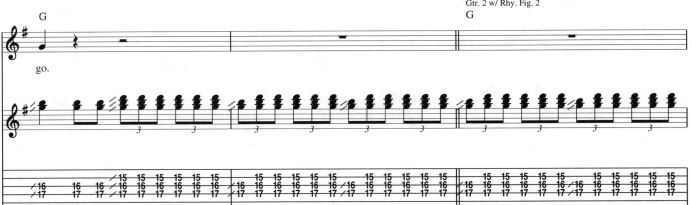

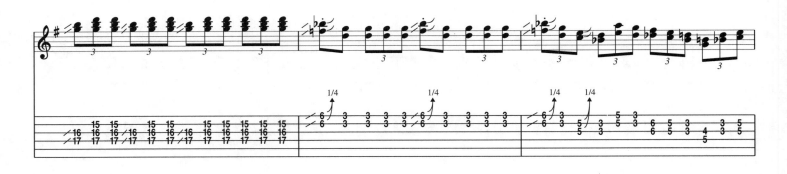

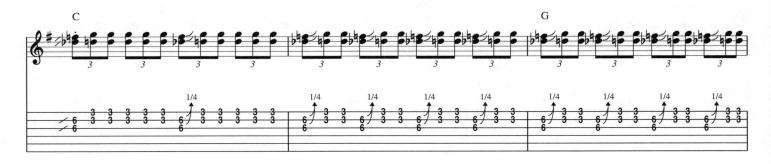

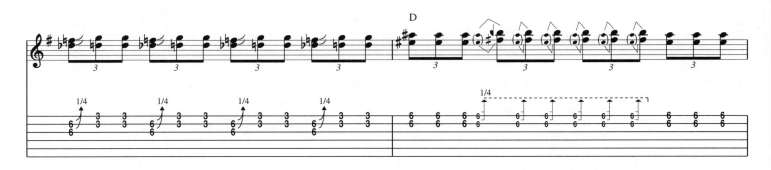

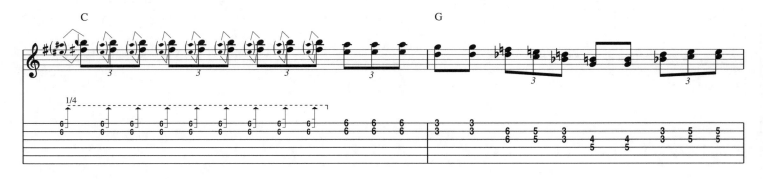

130

Gtr. 2: w/ Rhy. Fig. 2, 1st 10 meas.

Paranoid

Words and Music by Anthony Iommi, John Osbourne, William Ward and Terence Butler

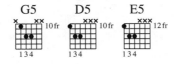

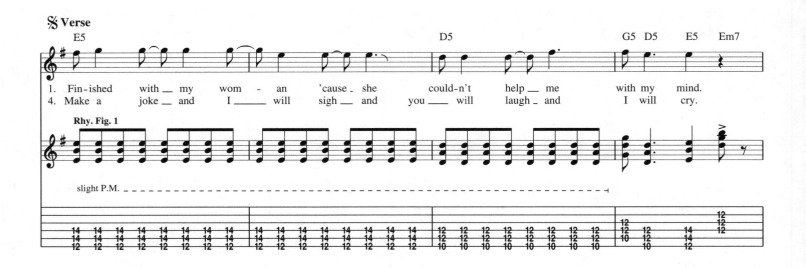

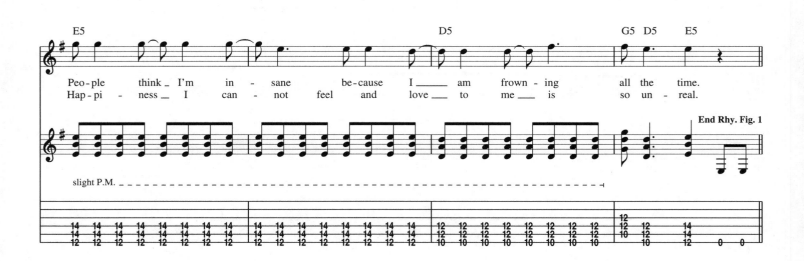

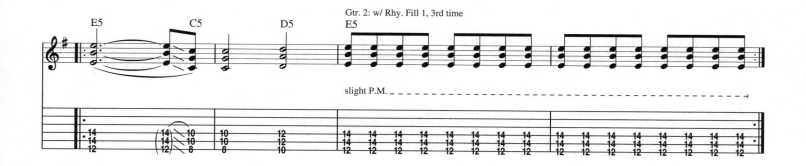

Verse

2. All day long ___ I think ___ of things ___ but noth - ing seems ___ to sat - is - fy.
5. And so as ___ you hear ___ these words ___ tell - ing you now _____ of ___ my state.

Think I'll lose ___ my mind ___ if I ____ don't find ___ some - thing ___ to pass it by.
I tell you ___ to en - joy life, ___ I wish ___ I could ___ but it's too late.

Bridge

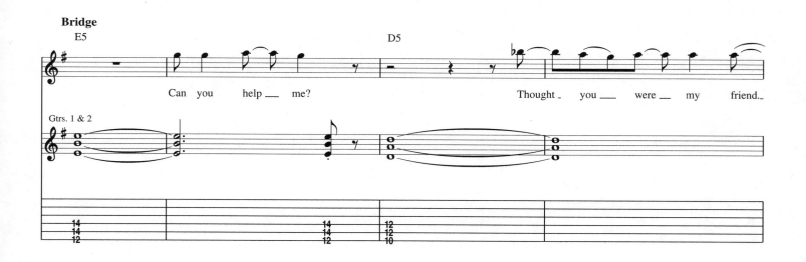

Can you help ___ me?   Thought ___ you ___ were ___ my friend. __

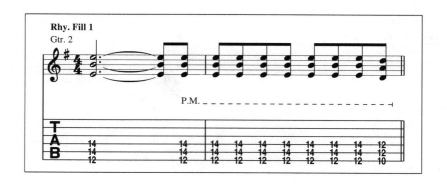

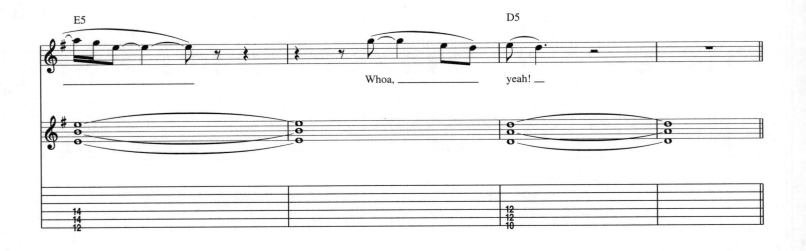

Whoa, _____ yeah! _____

Interlude

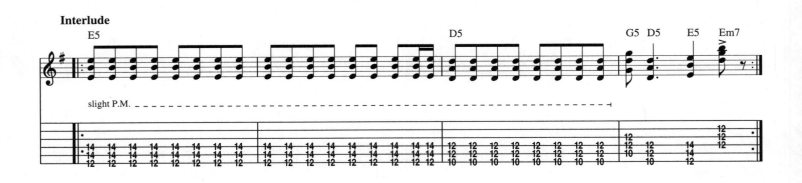

slight P.M. -

Verse

Gtrs. 1 & 2: w/ Rhy. Fig. 1

3. I need some - one to ___ show me ___ the things ___ in life ___ that I can't find.

I can't see ___ the things ___ that make ___ true hap - pi - ness, ___ I must be blind.

Guitar Solo

Gtr. 2: w/ Rhy. Fig. 1, 1st 4 meas., 4 times

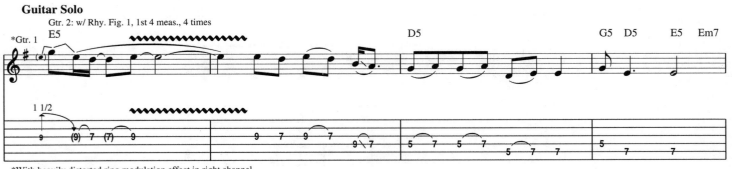

*With heavily distorted ring modulation effect in right channel.

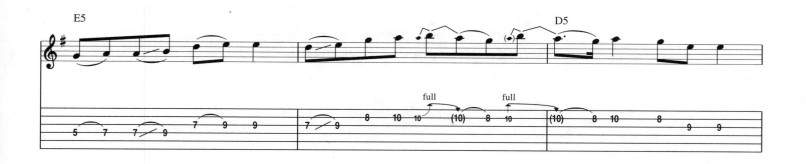

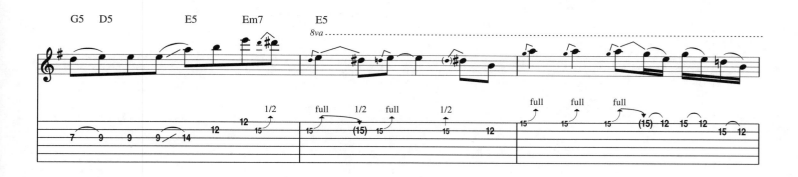

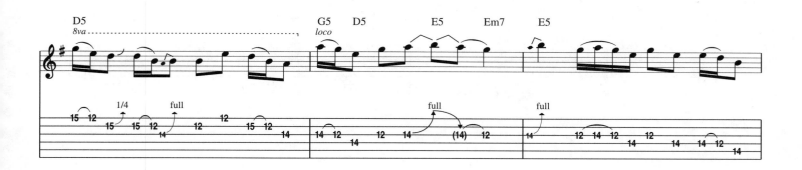

Interlude   *D.S. al Coda*
Gtrs. 1 & 2: w/ Rhy. Fig. 1,
1st 4 meas., 2 times

✛ *Coda*
Outro
Gtrs. 1 & 2: w/ Rhy. Fig. 1, 1st 7 meas.

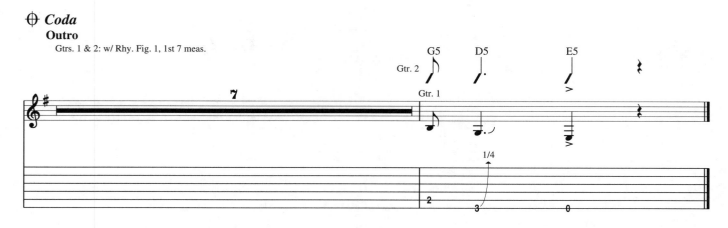

Piece of My Heart

Words and Music by Bert Berns and Jerry Ragovoy

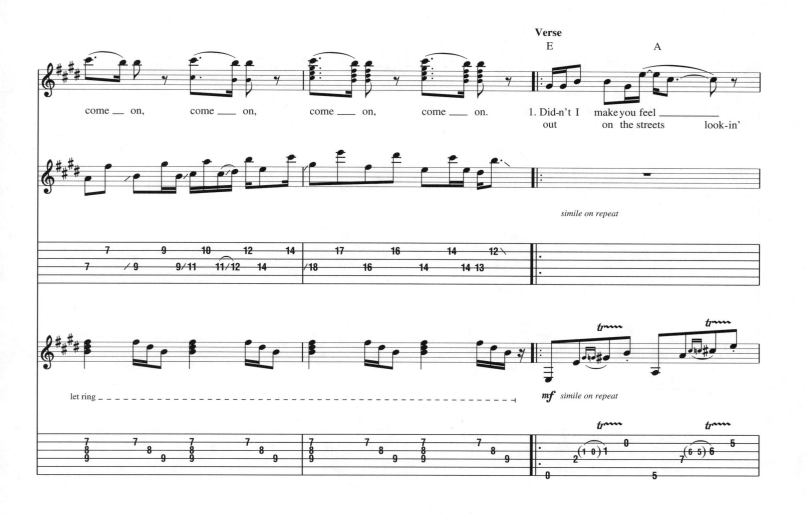

come __ on, come __ on, come __ on, come __ on.

1. Did-n't I make you feel
out on the streets look-in'

simile on repeat

let ring ------------------- *mf* *simile on repeat*

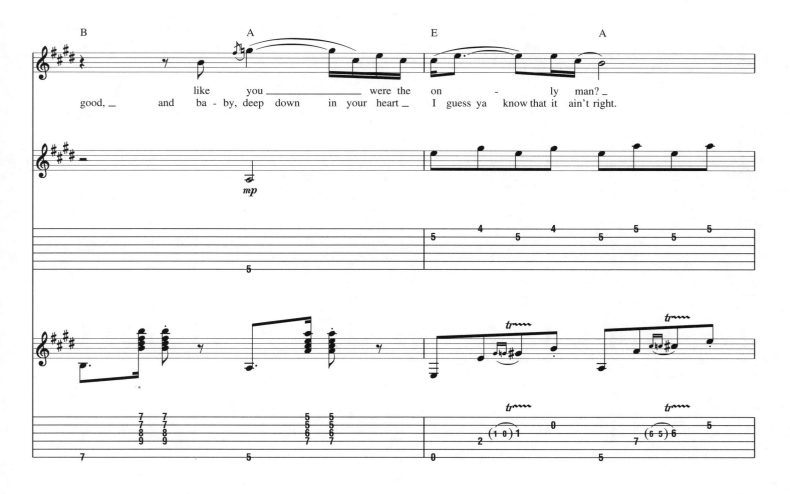

like you _____ were the on - ly man? __
good, __ and ba - by, deep down in your heart __ I guess ya know that it ain't right.

mp

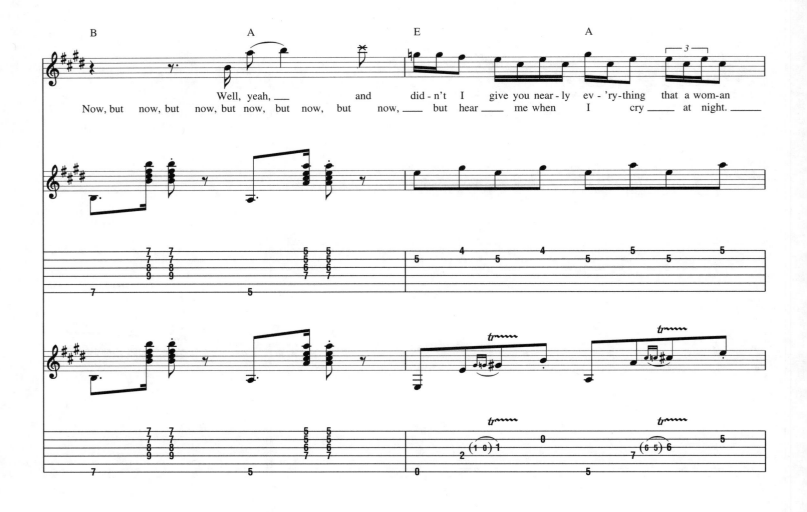

Well, yeah, ___ and did-n't I give you near-ly ev-'ry-thing that a wom-an
Now, but now, but now, but now, but now, but now, ___ but hear ___ me when I cry ___ at night. ___

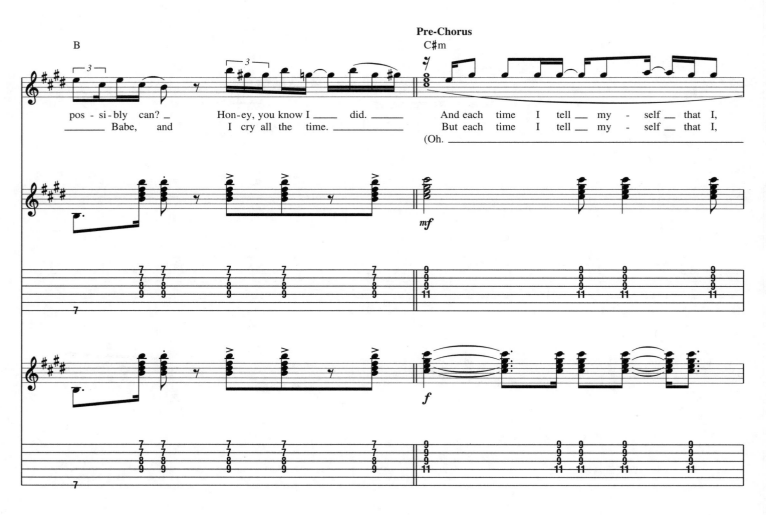

pos - si - bly can? _ Hon-ey, you know I ___ did. ___ And each time I tell ___ my - self ___ that I,
___ Babe, and I cry all the time. ___ But each time I tell ___ my - self ___ that I,
(Oh. ___

Pre-Chorus

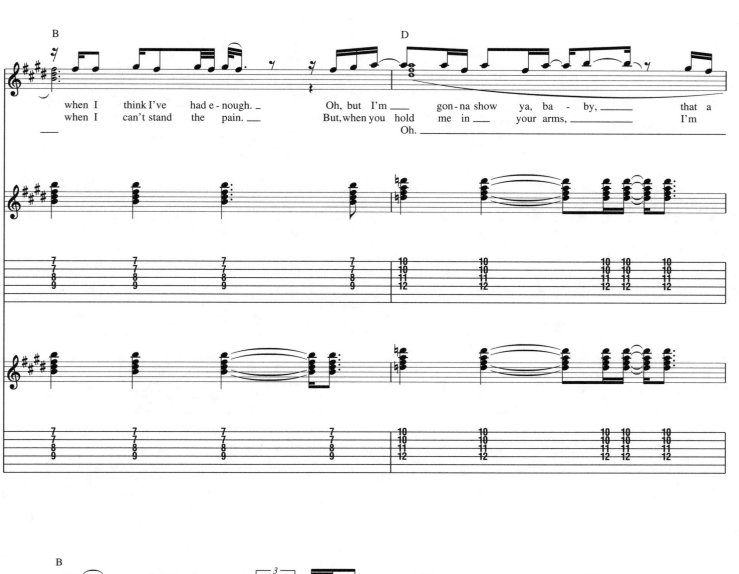

when I   think I've   had e - nough. __   Oh, but I'm __   gon-na show   ya, ba - by, _____   that a
when I   can't stand   the   pain. __   But, when you hold   me in __   your arms, _____   I'm
__   Oh. _____

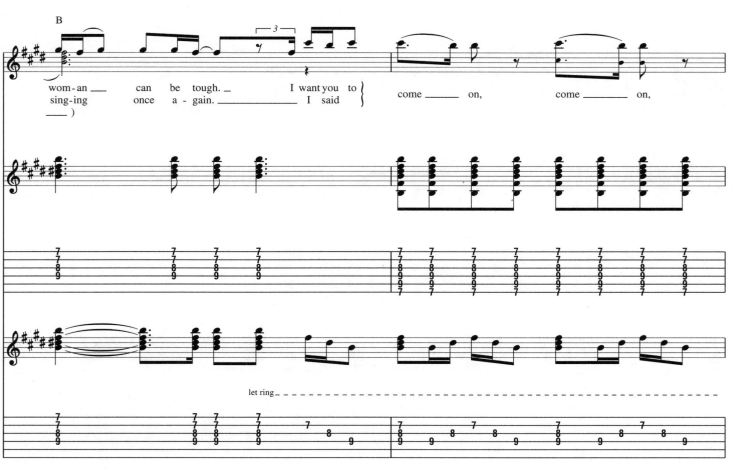

wom-an __   can   be   tough. __   I want you to ⎫   come _____   on,   come _____   on,
sing-ing   once   a - gain. _____   I said ⎬
__   ⎠

let ring _

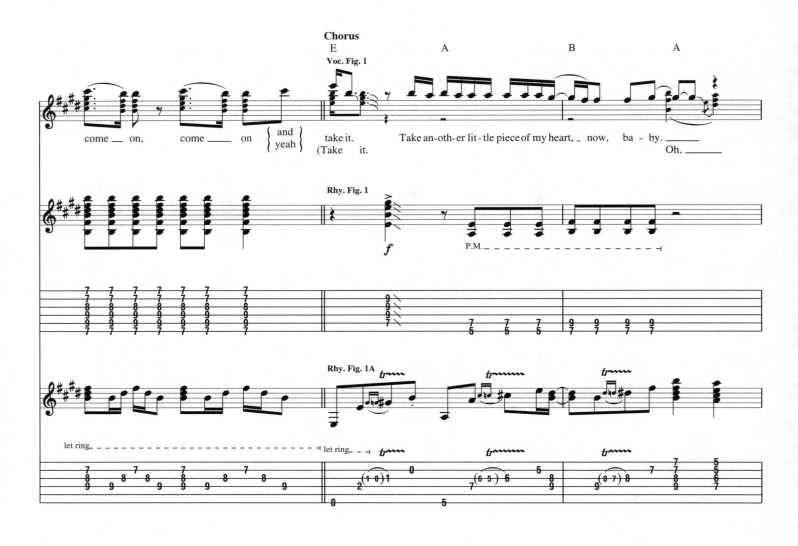

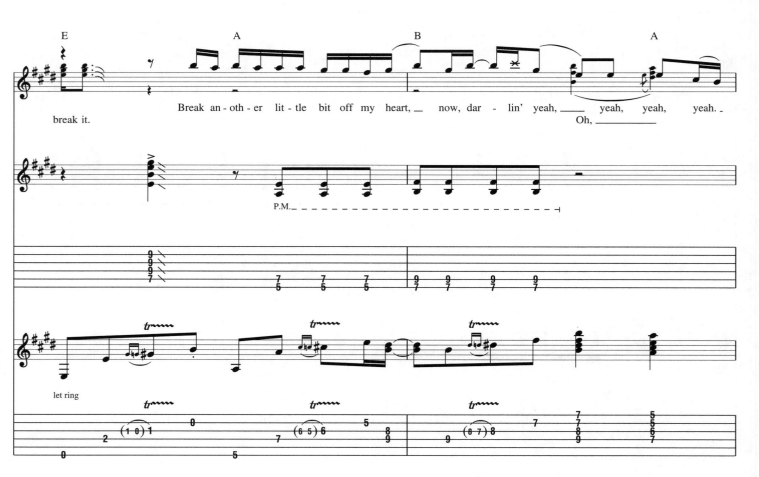

Have an-oth-er lit-tle piece of my heart, __ now, ba-by. __ Well, you know you got __ it if it

have a...)

makes you feel good, __ oh, yes in-deed. __

2. You're

Chorus

take it.   Take an - oth - er   lit - tle piece of my heart, _____ now, ba - by. _____

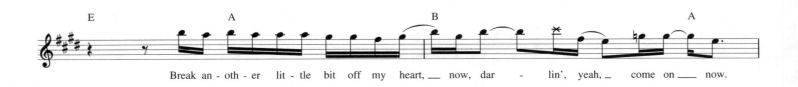

Break an - oth - er   lit - tle bit off my heart, __ now, dar - lin', yeah, __ come on __ now.

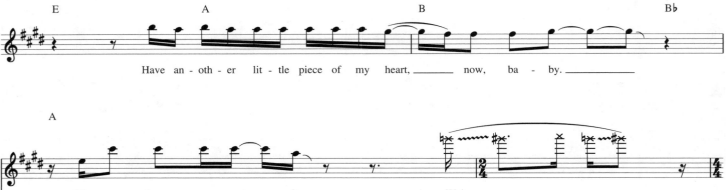

Have an - oth - er   lit - tle piece of my heart, _____ now, ba - by. _____

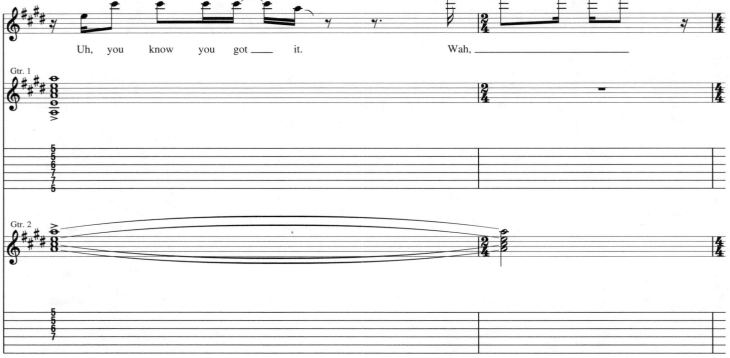

Uh, you   know   you got ___ it.   Wah, _____

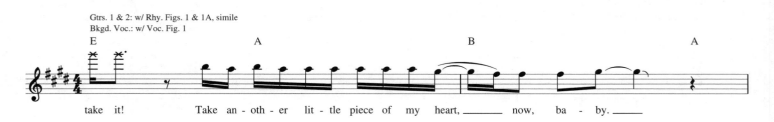

take it!   Take an - oth - er   lit - tle piece of my heart, _____ now, ba - by. _____

Reeling in the Years

Words and Music by Walter Becker and Donald Fagen

think is gon-na   last.__ Well you would-n't e-ven know a dia-mond if you held it in your hand.   The

things you think are pre-cious I can't un-der-stand.   Are you reel-in' in the

End Riff A

End Riff A1

Chorus

Gtr. 3 tacet

years; ___   stow-in' a-way the   time? ___   Are you gath-er-in' up the

Gtr. 2   **Rhy. Fig. 1**

148

tears? ___   Have you had e-nough of mine? ___   Are you reel-in' in the

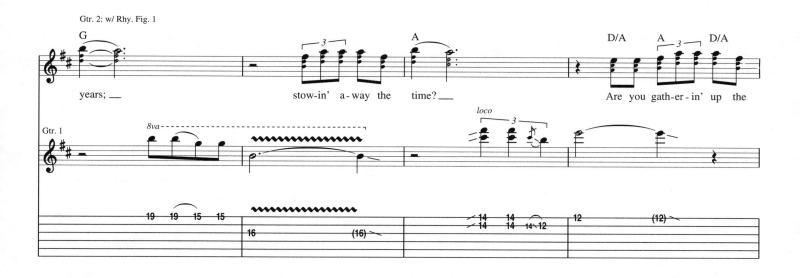

years; ___   stow-in' a-way the time? ___   Are you gath-er-in' up the

tears? ___   Have you had e-nough of mine? ___

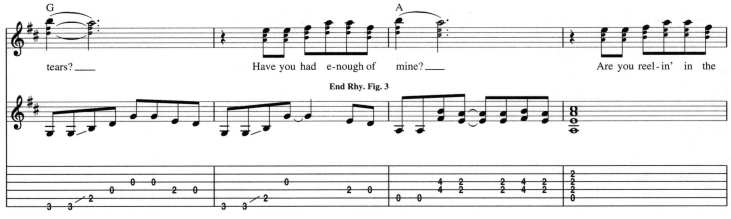

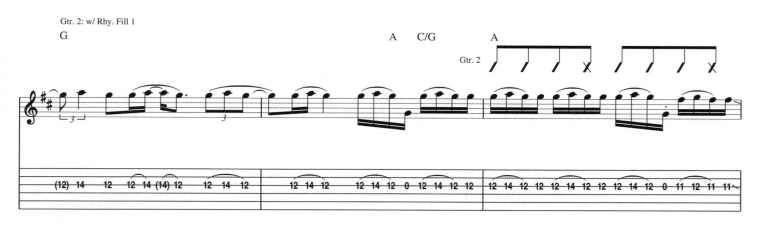

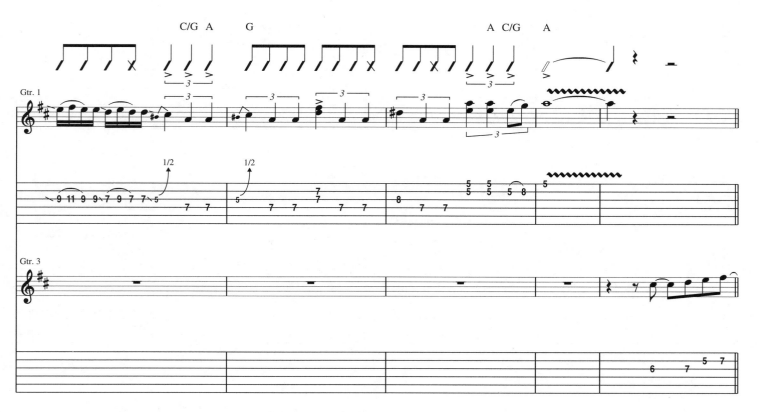

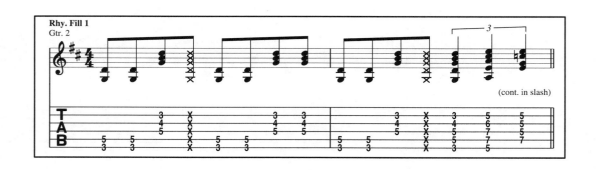

Are you gath-er-in' up the tears? ___ Have you had e-nough of

mine? ___

Interlude

Gtr. 2: w/ Riff B

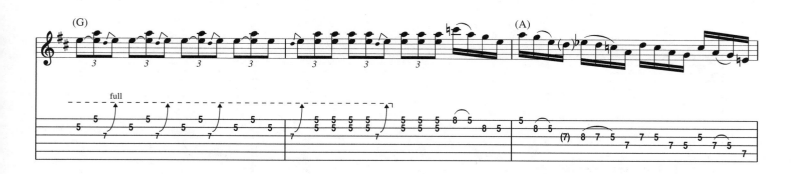

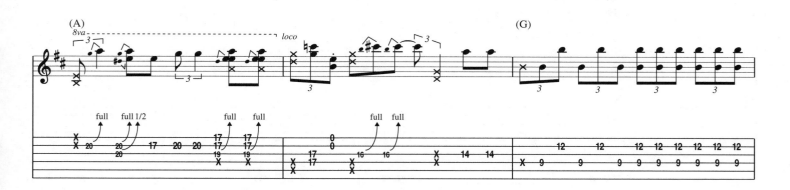

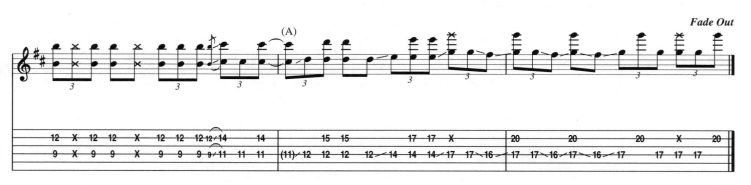

Rock and Roll All Nite

Words and Music by Paul Stanley and Gene Simmons

Tune down 1/2 step:

(low to high) Eb-Ab-Db-Gb-Bb-Eb

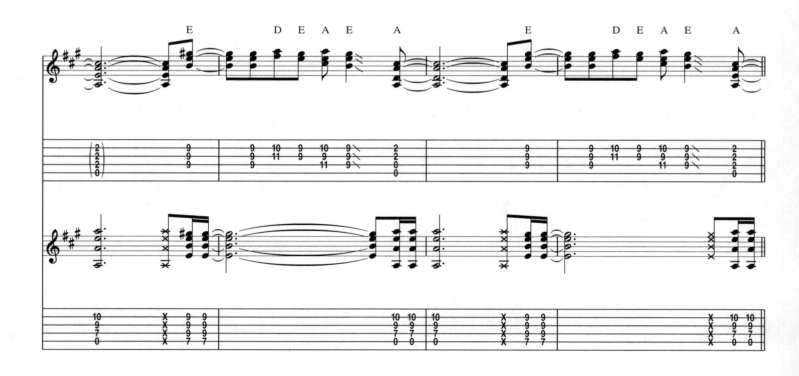

*Chord symbols reflect combined harmony.

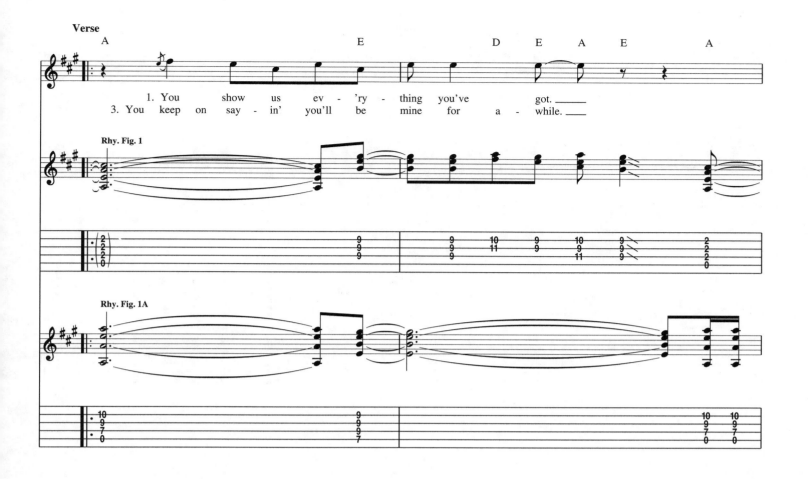

1. You show us ev - 'ry - thing you've got. ____
3. You keep on say - in' you'll be mine for a - while. ____

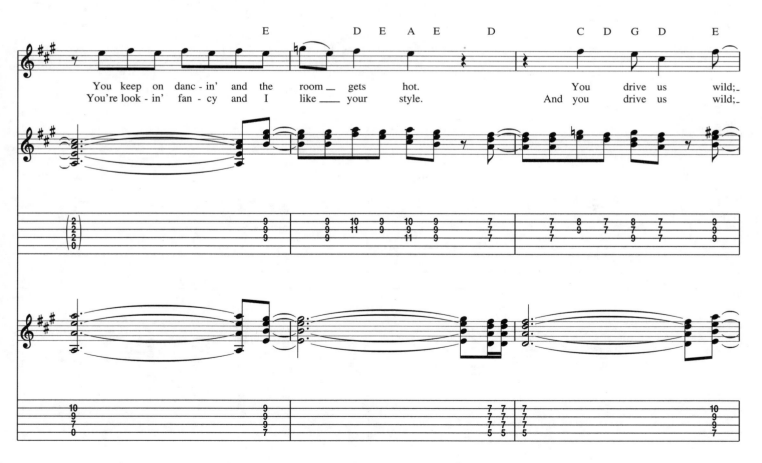

You keep on danc - in' and the room __ gets hot. You drive us wild; __
You're look - in' fan - cy and I like __ your style. And you drive us wild; __

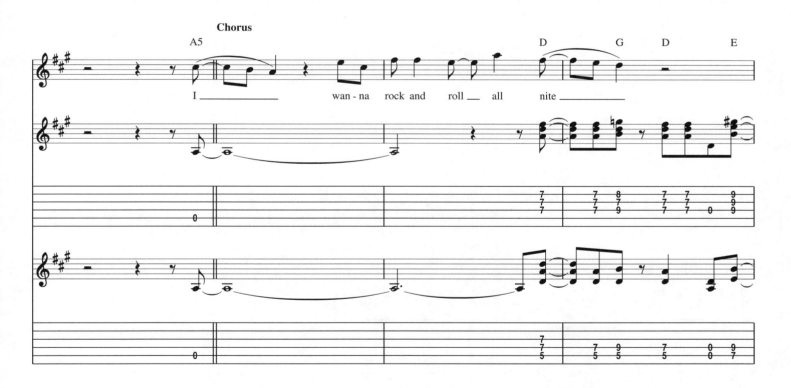

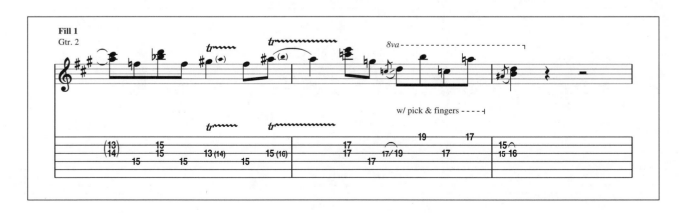

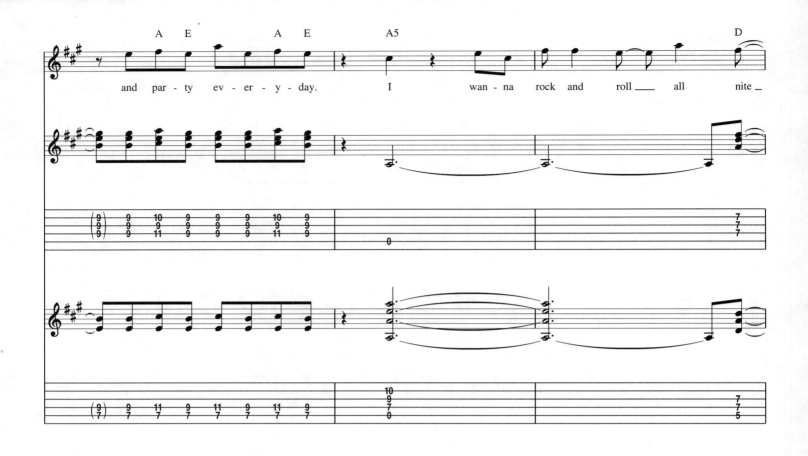

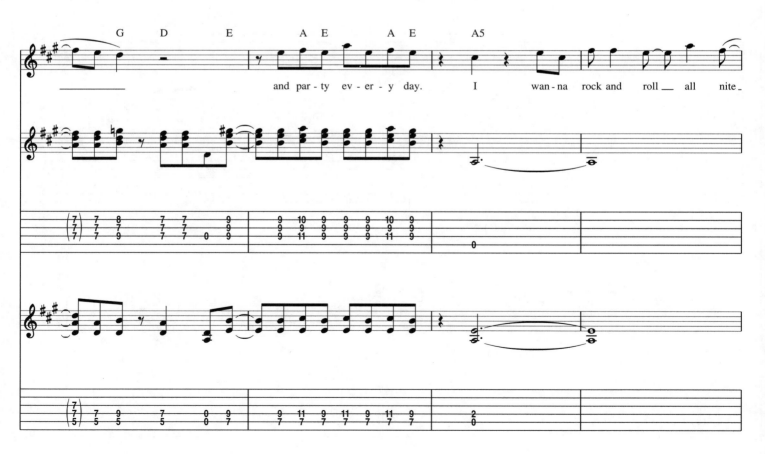

and par - ty ev - er - y day. I wan - na rock and roll ___ all nite ___

To Coda ⊕
Gtrs. 1 & 2: w/ Rhy. Fills 1 & 1A

and par - ty ev - er - y day.

Guitar Solo

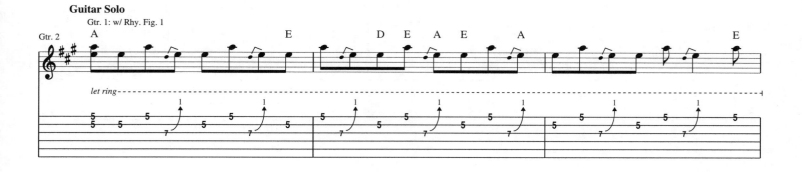

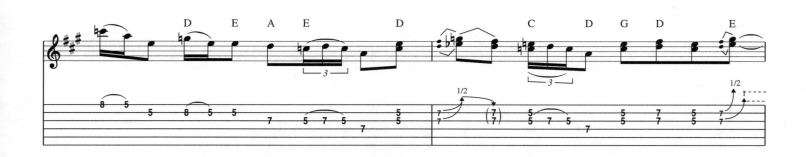

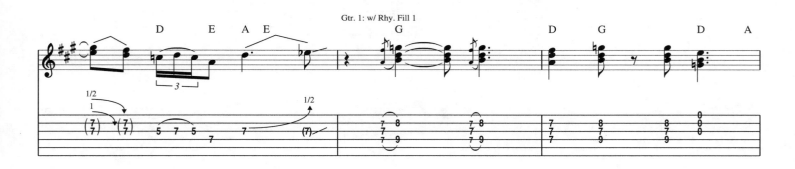

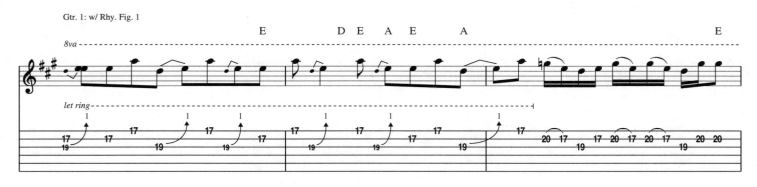

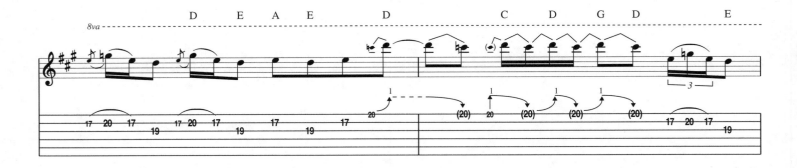

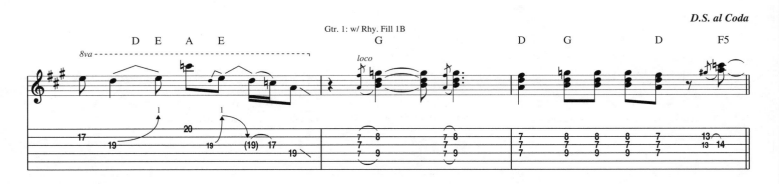

D.S. al Coda

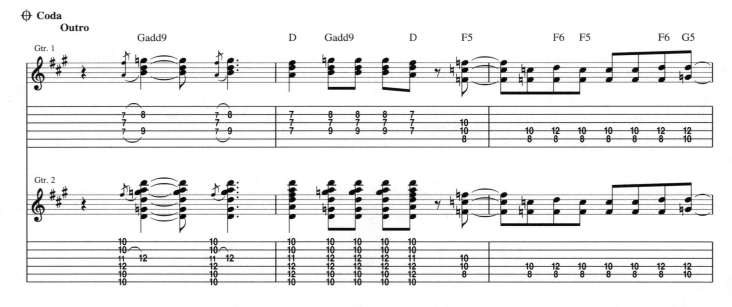

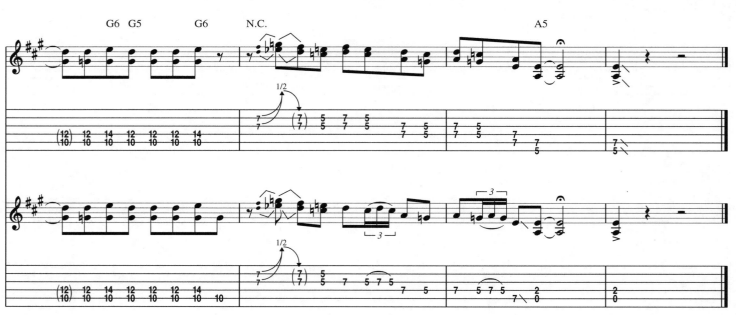

Saturday Night's Alright (For Fighting)

Words and Music by Elton John and Bernie Taupin

na rock.　　　　Wan-na get＿ a bel-ly full of beer.＿　　My
what I need.　　I can sink a lit-tle drink and shout out "She's with me!"　　A

End Rhy. Fig. 1

Gtr. 1

Gtr. 2

mf

Gtr. 1: w/ Rhy. Fig. 1
Gtr. 2 tacet

old man's a drunk-er than a bar-rel full of mon-keys and my ol' la-dy she don't care.＿
cou-ple of the sounds that I real-ly＿ like are the sounds of a switch-blade and a

My sis-ter looks cute in her britch-es and boots.＿　　Whose
mo-tor bike.　I'm a ju-ve-nile prod-uct of the work-ing class.＿　　A

simile on repeat

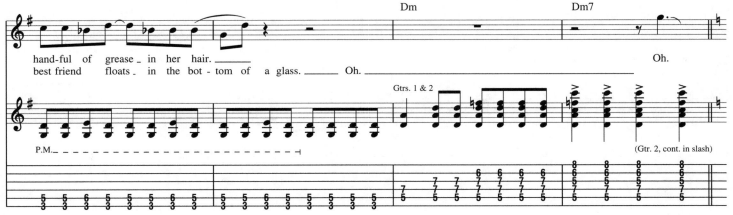

hand-ful of grease＿ in her hair.＿　　　　　　　　Oh.
best friend floats＿ in the bot-tom of a glass.＿＿ Oh.＿＿＿＿＿＿＿＿

Gtrs. 1 & 2

P.M. ＿＿＿＿＿＿＿＿＿　　　　　　　　　　　　　(Gtr. 2, cont. in slash)

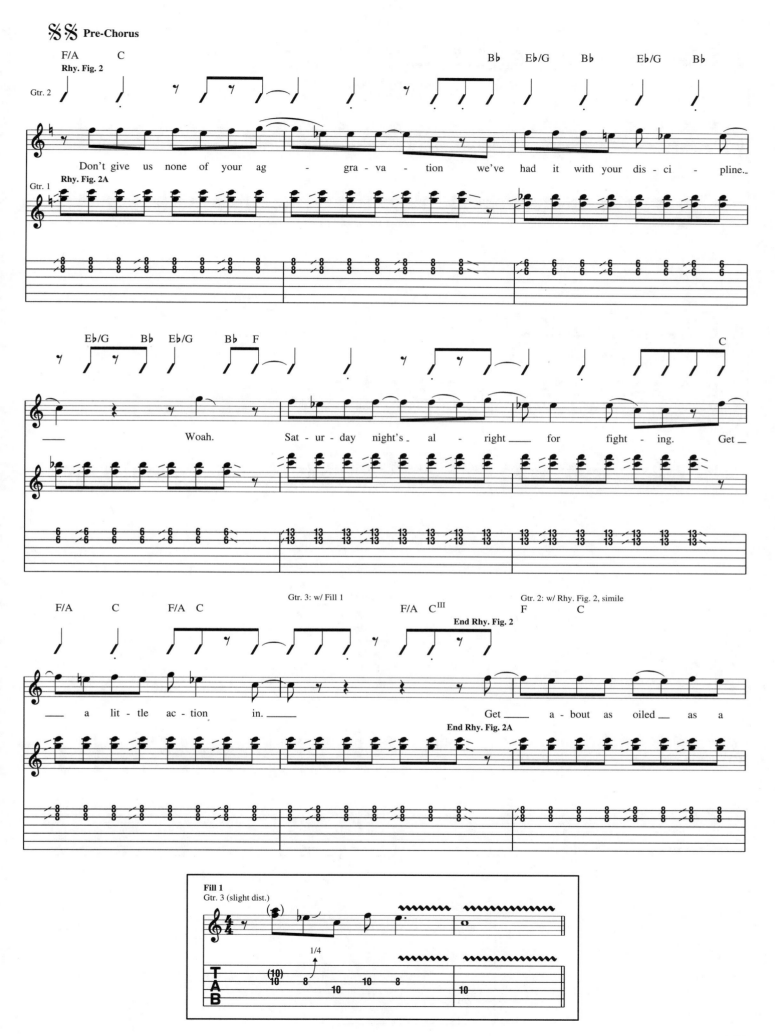

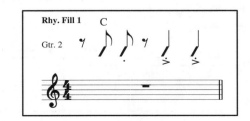

2. Well they're

⊕ Coda 1

Interlude

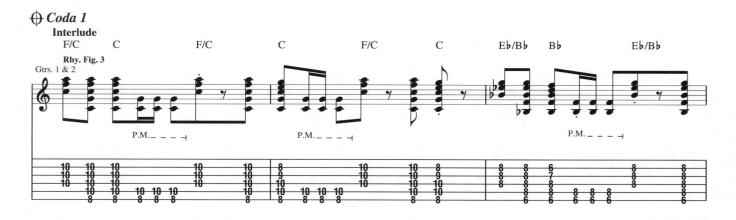

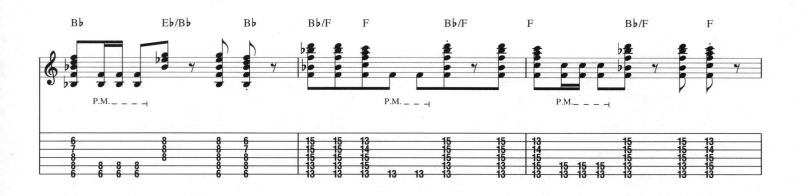

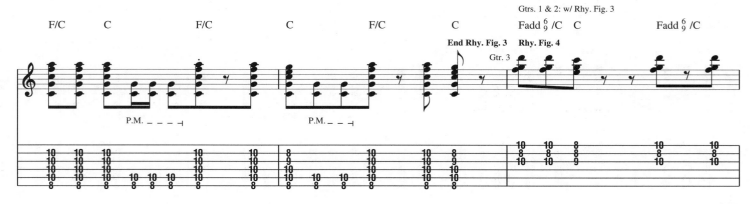

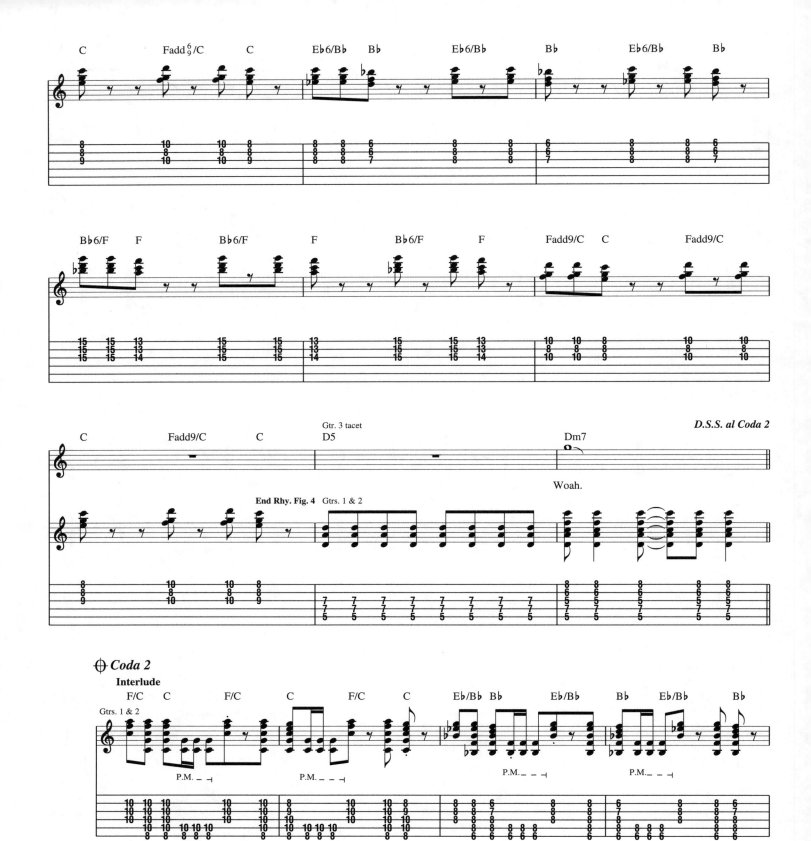

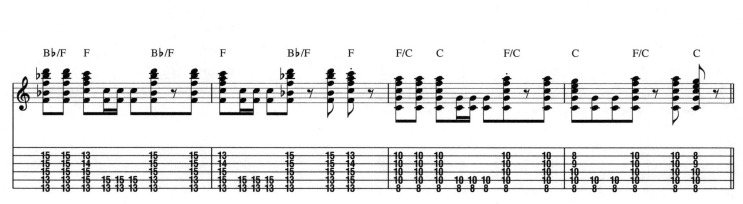

Chorus

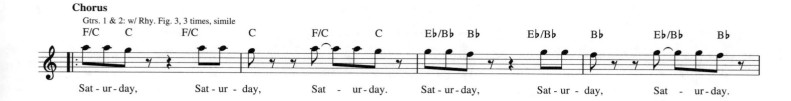

Outro

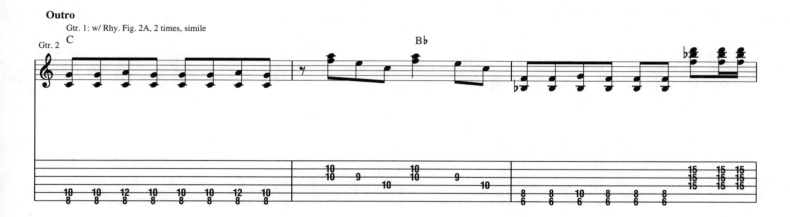

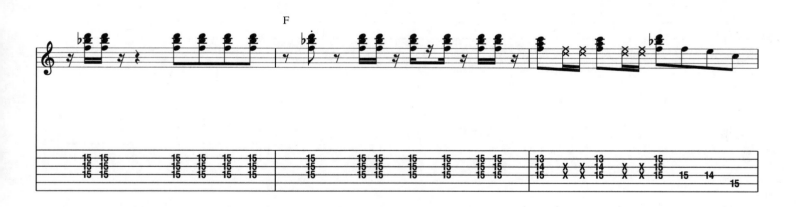

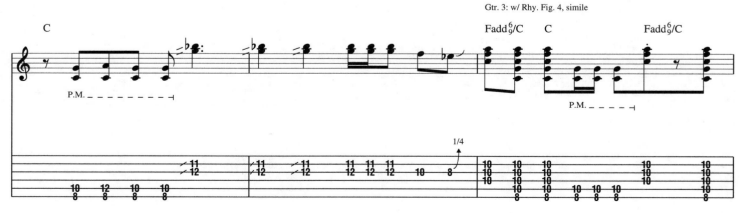

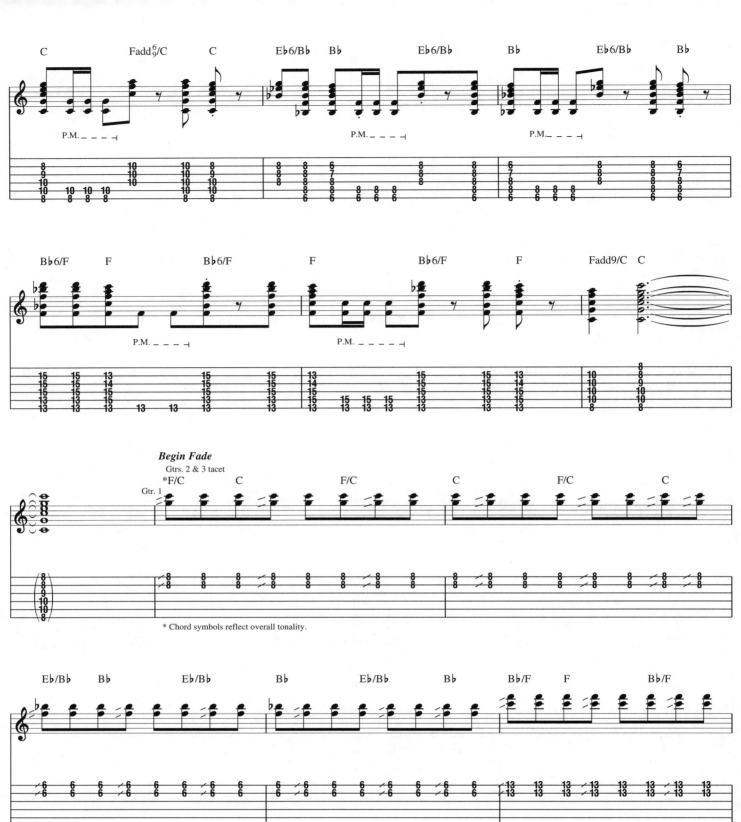

* Chord symbols reflect overall tonality.

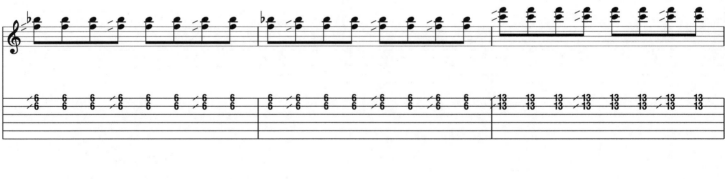

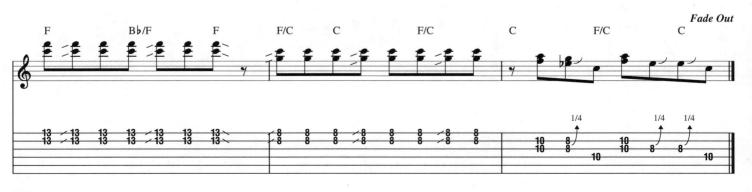

Substitute

Words and Music by Peter Townshend

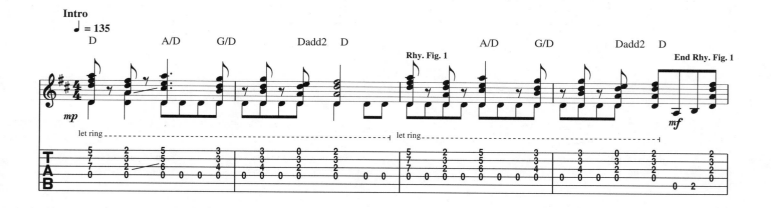

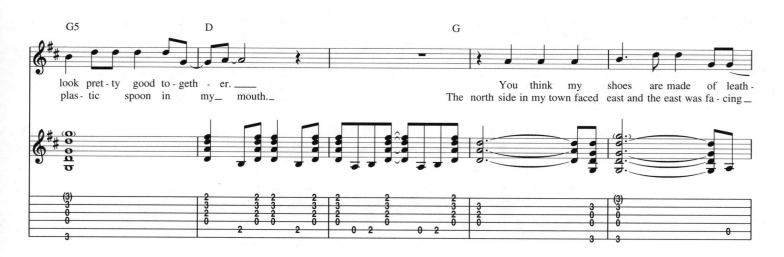

Pre-Chorus
w/ Rhy. Fill 1, 2nd time, 7 times

I'm a sub-sti-tute___ for a-noth-er guy. I
Now you dare to look me in the eye. Those

look pret-ty tall but my heels are high. The sim-ple things ya' see are all com-pli-ca-ted. (I
croc-o-dile tears are what you cry. It's a gen-u-ine prob-lem. You won't try___ to

look blood-y young but I'm just back-dat-ed, yeah.
work it out at all; you just pass it by, pass it by.___

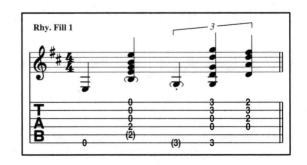

Rhy. Fill 1

174

Chorus

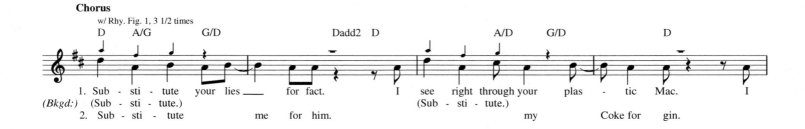

1. Sub - sti - tute your lies ___ for fact. I see right through your plas - tic Mac. I
(Bkgd:) (Sub - sti - tute.)   (Sub - sti - tute.)
2. Sub - sti - tute me for him.   my Coke for gin.

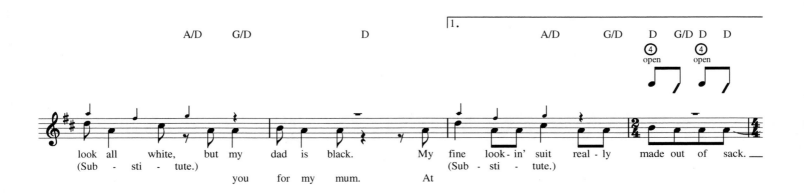

look all white, but my dad is black. My fine look - in' suit real - ly made out of sack. ___
(Sub - sti - tute.)   (Sub - sti - tute.)
          you for my mum. At

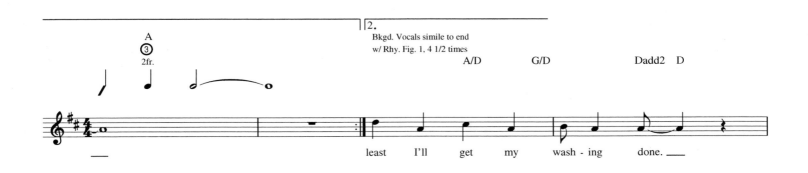

least I'll get my wash - ing done. ___

mp Sub - sti - tute your lies ___ for fact. I see right through your plas - tic Mac. I   *mf*

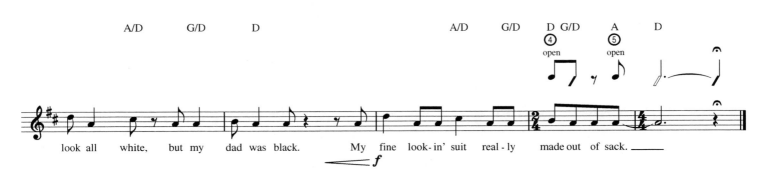

look all white, but my dad was black. My fine look - in' suit real - ly made out of sack. _____
          f

Sultans of Swing

Words and Music by Mark Knopfler

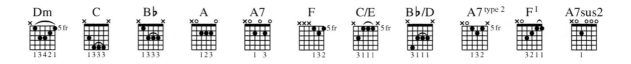

south of the riv-er you stop, and you hold _____ ev-'ry-thing.

A band is blow-ing Dix-ie dou-ble four ___ time,

you feel al-right when you hear the mu-sic ___ ring.

let ring

(cont. in notation)

(cont. in slash)

177

4. And Har-ry does-n't mind   if he does-n't   make the scene, __

he's got a day-time job,   he's do-ing al - right.

Verse

Gtr. 2: w/ Rhy. Fig. 4, simile

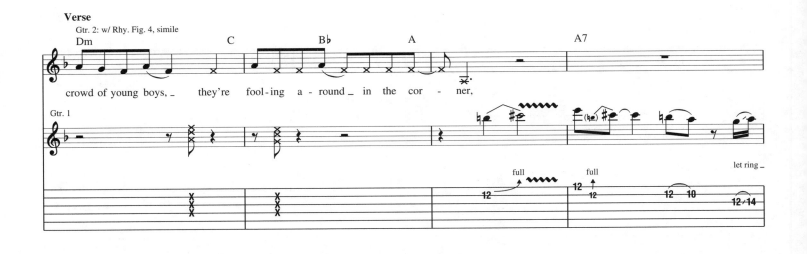

crowd of young boys, _ they're fool-ing a-round _ in the cor - ner,

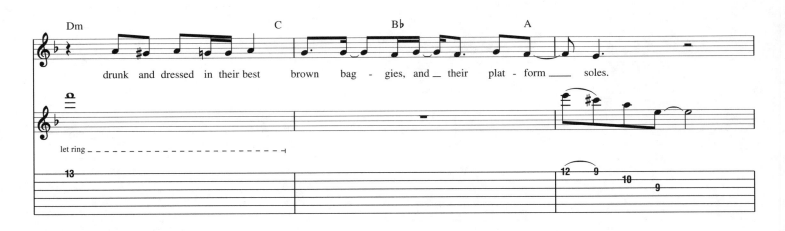

drunk and dressed in their best brown bag - gies, and _ their plat-form _ soles.

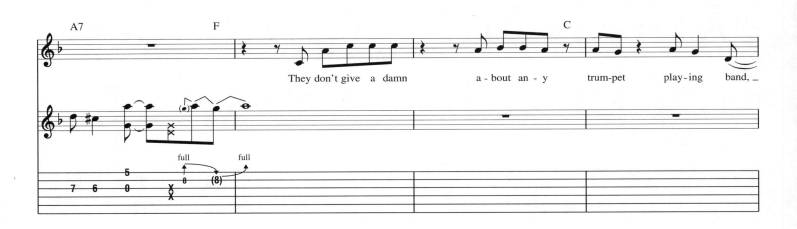

They don't give a damn a-bout an-y trum-pet play-ing band, _

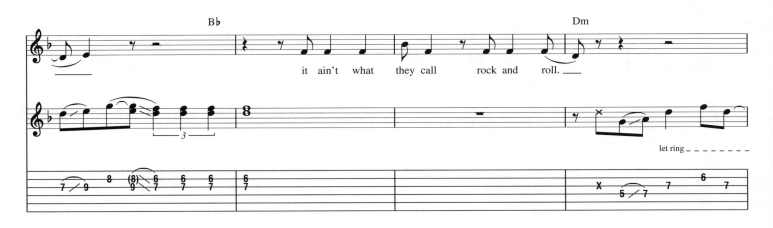

it ain't what they call rock and roll. _

Sunshine of Your Love

Words and Music by Jack Bruce, Pete Brown and Eric Clapton

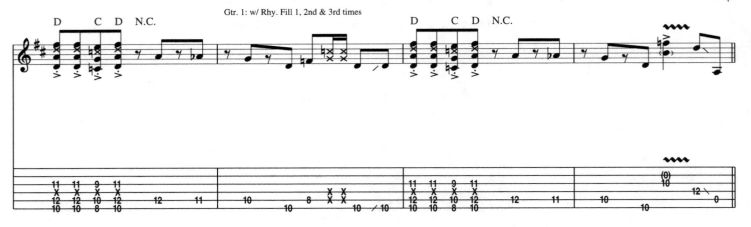

Chorus

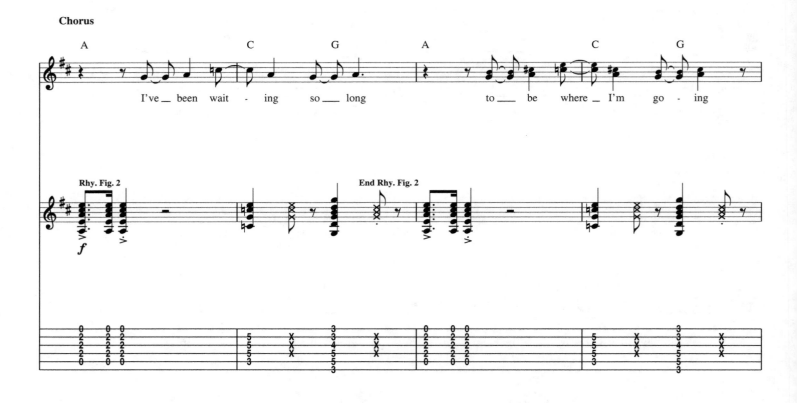

I've __ been wait - ing so __ long   to __ be where __ I'm go - ing

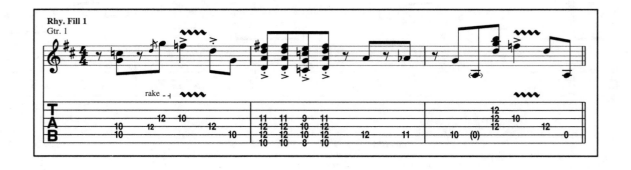

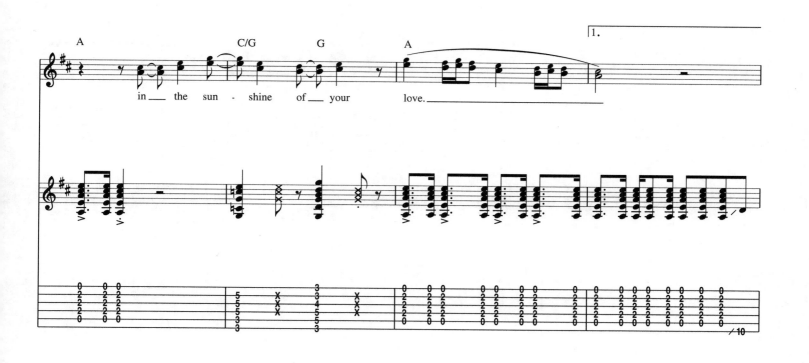

in __ the sun - shine of __ your love. _____

2. I'm __

Guitar Solo

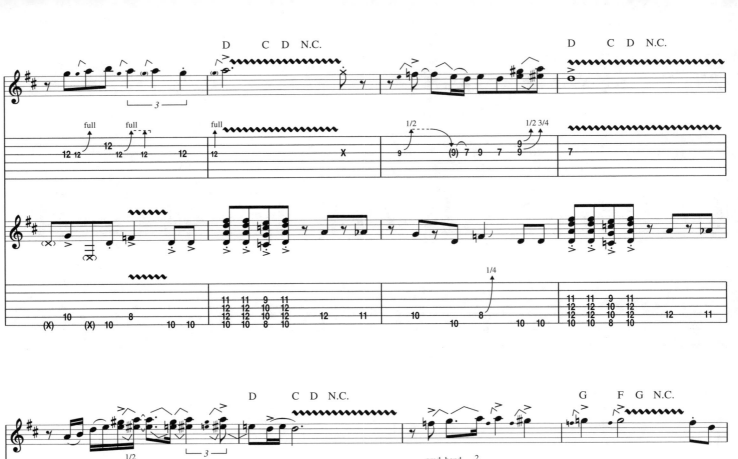

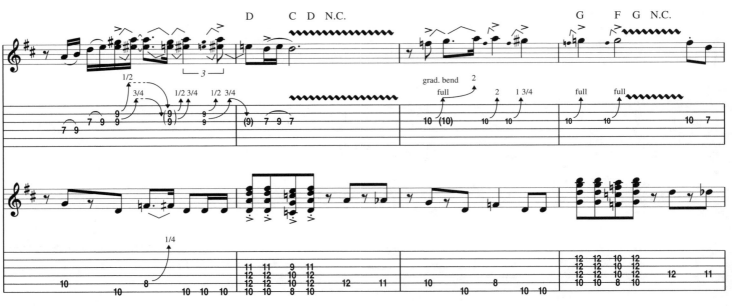

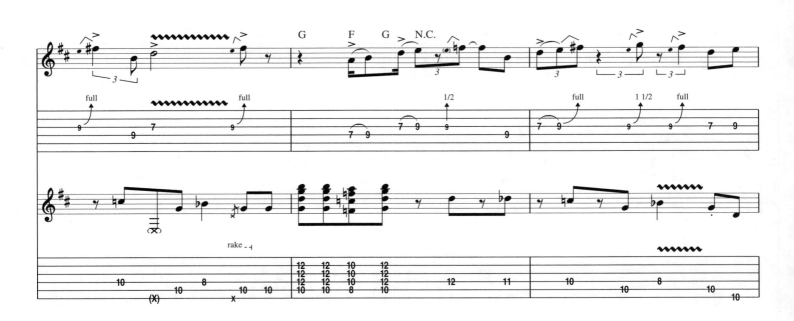

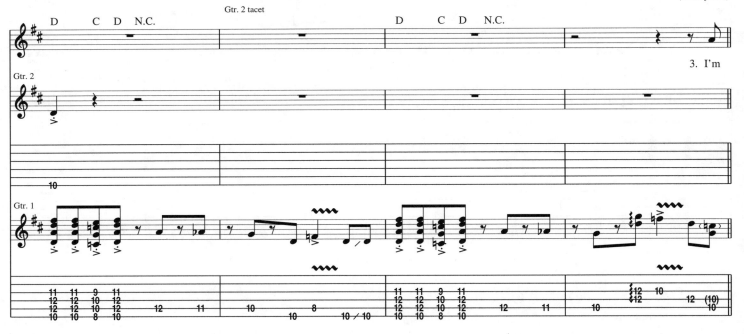

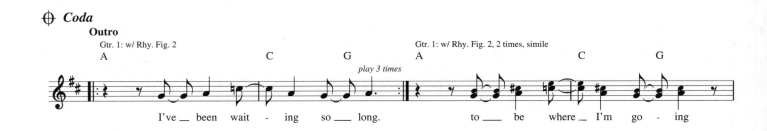

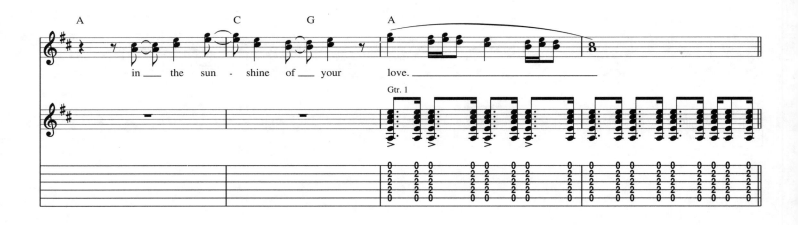

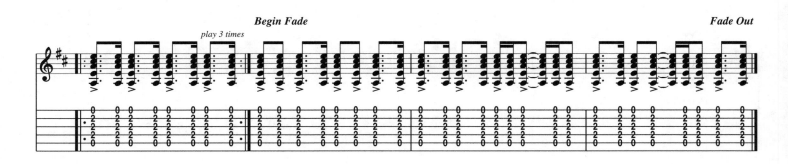

194

Susie-Q

Words and Music by Dale Hawkins, Stan Lewis and Eleanor Broadwater

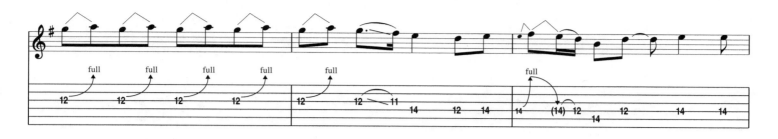

Gtr. 2: w/ Rhy. Fig. 3

Gtr. 2: w/ Rhy. Fig. 1
Gtr. 3: w/ Fill 1

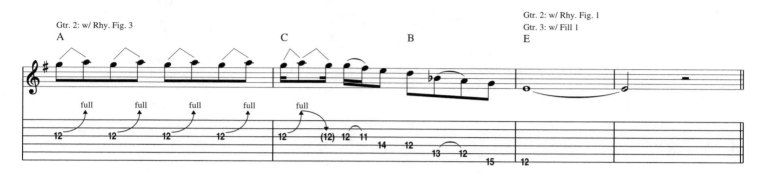

1., 2., 3. | 4.

D.S. al Coda 1

Interlude

Gtr. 2: w/ Rhy. Fig. 1
Em7

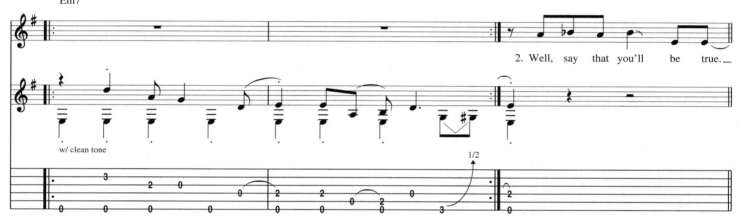

2. Well, say that you'll be true.

w/ clean tone

$\oplus$ *Coda 1*

Guitar Solo

Gtr. 2: w/ Rhy. Fig. 1, 4 times
E

Gtr. 1

let ring

let ring

Fill 1
Gtr. 3

* *mf* *f* *mf* *dim.*

w/ fast tremolo

*fade in

197

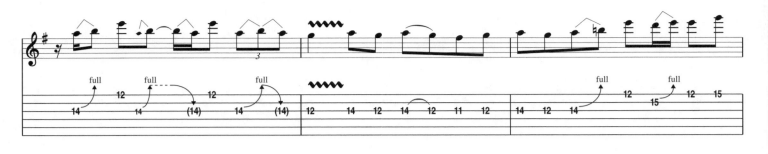

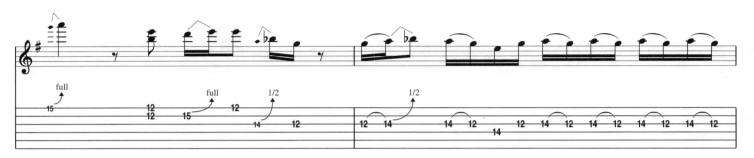

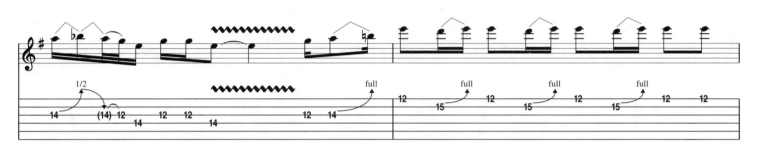

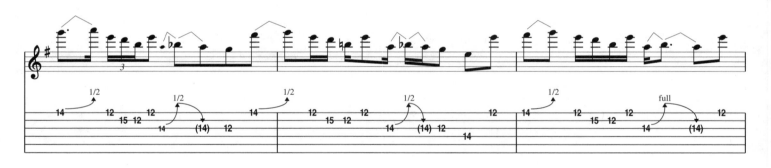

Begin Fade

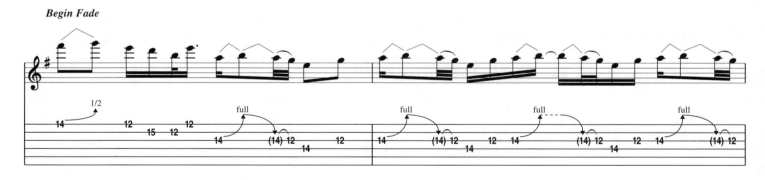

Fade Out

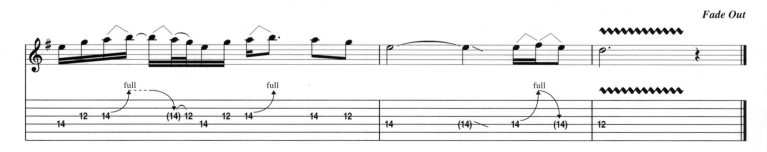

Takin' Care of Business

Words and Music by Randy Bachman

206

Walk This Way

Words and Music by Steven Tyler and Joe Perry

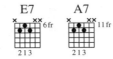

ain't   seen   noth-in'   till you're   down   on   a   muf-fin   and you're   sure   to   be   a-chang-in' your ways."   I   met   a

three   young   la - dies   in the school   gym   lock-er   when   I   no-ticed   they was   look-in'   at   me.   I   was   a

cheer - lead - er,   was   a   real   young   bleed-er   all   the   times   I   could   rem - i -   nisce,   'cause the

high   school   los-er,   nev-er   made   it   with   a   la-dy   'til   the   boys   told   me   some-thin'   I   missed,   then   my

best   things   in   lov-in'   with   a   sis-ter   and   a   cou-sin   on - ly   start-ed   with   a   lit - tle   kiss,   a - like   this!

next   door   neigh-bor   with   a   daugh-ter   had   a   fav - or   so   I   gave   her   just   a   lit - tle   kiss   a - like   this!

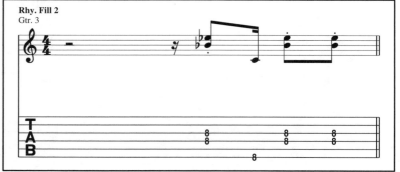

Interlude

Gtr. 1: w/ Riff A, 2nd time

N.C.(E5)

Gtr. 1

Gtr. 2
divisi

Gtr. 3: w/ Rhy. Fill 1

Gtrs. 1 & 2

A5

Verse

Gtrs. 1 & 2: w/ Rhy. Fig. 1, 3 times, simile

N.C.(C7)

2., 4. See - saw swing-in' with the boys in the school and your feet fly - in' up in the air, ___ I sing,

"Hey did - dle did - dle" with your kit - ty in the mid - dle of the swing like you did - n't care. ___ So I

took a big chance at the high school dance with a miss - y who was read - y to play, ___ was a

* Sing harmony 1st time only.

Riff A

Gtr. 1

P.M. ⌐ ⌐ ⌐ ⌐ ⌐ ⌐

P.M. ⌐ ⌐ ⌐ ⌐

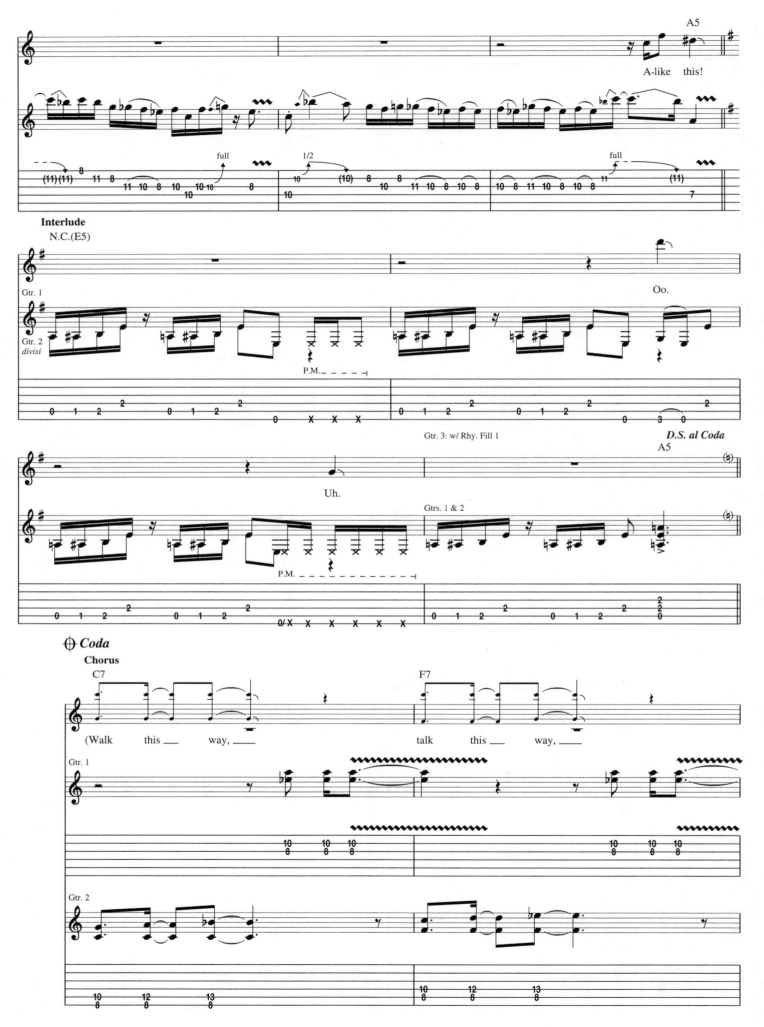

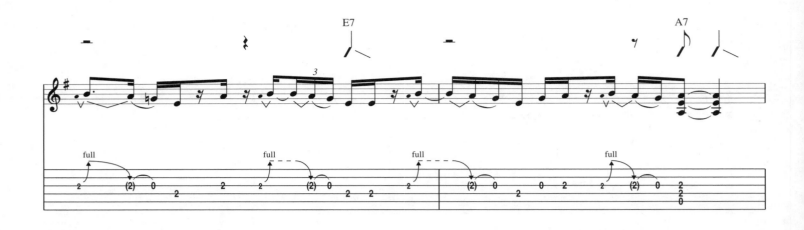

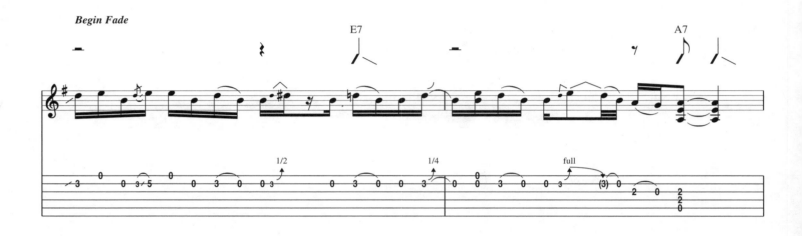

Begin Fade

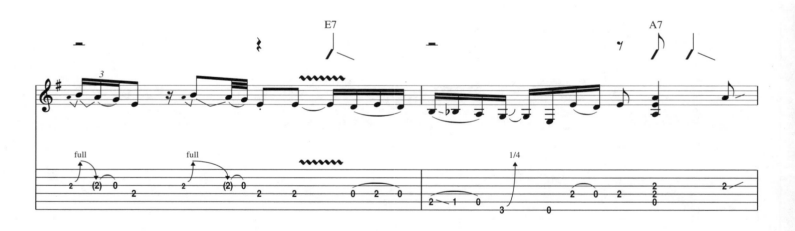

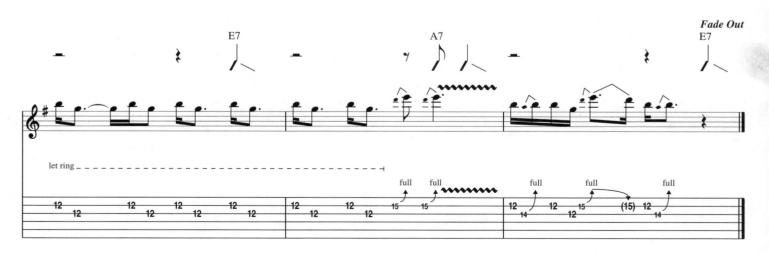

216

You Really Got Me

Words and Music by Ray Davies

*Flick toggle switch between on & off pickup
 selection to create specified rhythm. Rhythm shown
 is only for the "on" position sound.

Interlude

Gtr. 1 tacet
N.C.

Ah. ___   Ah. ___   Ah. ___ Ah. ___   Ah. ___
(Ah,   ah,   ah,   ah.   Ah, ah.   Chu, chu, chu, chu, chu, ch, ch.)

Verse

w/ ad lib vocal effects
N.C.

3. Girl,   you real - ly got me now,   you got me so I don't know what I'm do - in'. ___

___   Ah.   Girl, you real - ly got me now, _   you got me so I can't sleep at night! ___

Girl,   you real - ly got me now, _   you got me so I don't know where I'm go - in', ___
(Girl, _____

Guitar Notation Legend

Guitar Music can be notated three different ways: on a *musical staff*, in *tablature*, and in *rhythm slashes*.

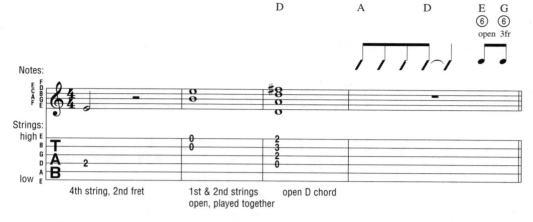

RHYTHM SLASHES are written above the staff. Strum chords in the rhythm indicated. Use the chord diagrams found at the top of the first page of the transcription for the appropriate chord voicings. Round noteheads indicate single notes.

THE MUSICAL STAFF shows pitches and rhythms and is divided by bar lines into measures. Pitches are named after the first seven letters of the alphabet.

TABLATURE graphically represents the guitar fingerboard. Each horizontal line represents a a string, and each number represents a fret.

Definitions for Special Guitar Notation

HALF-STEP BEND: Strike the note and bend up 1/2 step.

WHOLE-STEP BEND: Strike the note and bend up one step.

GRACE NOTE BEND: Strike the note and immediately bend up as indicated.

SLIGHT (MICROTONE) BEND: Strike the note and bend up 1/4 step.

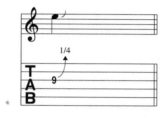

BEND AND RELEASE: Strike the note and bend up as indicated, then release back to the original note. Only the first note is struck.

PRE-BEND: Bend the note as indicated, then strike it.

PRE-BEND AND RELEASE: Bend the note as indicated. Strike it and release the bend back to the original note.

UNISON BEND: Strike the two notes simultaneously and bend the lower note up to the pitch of the higher.

VIBRATO: The string is vibrated by rapidly bending and releasing the note with the fretting hand.

WIDE VIBRATO: The pitch is varied to a greater degree by vibrating with the fretting hand.

HAMMER-ON: Strike the first (lower) note with one finger, then sound the higher note (on the same string) with another finger by fretting it without picking.

PULL-OFF: Place both fingers on the notes to be sounded. Strike the first note and without picking, pull the finger off to sound the second (lower) note.

LEGATO SLIDE: Strike the first note and then slide the same fret-hand finger up or down to the second note. The second note is not struck.

SHIFT SLIDE: Same as legato slide, except the second note is struck.

TRILL: Very rapidly alternate between the notes indicated by continuously hammering on and pulling off.

TAPPING: Hammer ("tap") the fret indicated with the pick-hand index or middle finger and pull off to the note fretted by the fret hand.

223

NATURAL HARMONIC: Strike the note while the fret-hand lightly touches the string directly over the fret indicated.

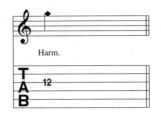

Harm.

T
A
B
12

PINCH HARMONIC: The note is fretted normally and a harmonic is produced by adding the edge of the thumb or the tip of the index finger of the pick hand to the normal pick attack.

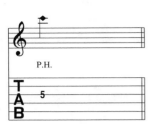

P.H.

T
A
B
5

HARP HARMONIC: The note is fretted normally and a harmonic is produced by gently resting the pick hand's index finger directly above the indicated fret (in parentheses) while the pick hand's thumb or pick assists by plucking the appropriate string.

8va

H.H.

T
A
B
7(19)

PICK SCRAPE: The edge of the pick is rubbed down (or up) the string, producing a scratchy sound.

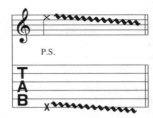

P.S.

MUFFLED STRINGS: A percussive sound is produced by laying the fret hand across the string(s) without depressing, and striking them with the pick hand.

T
A
B
X X
X X

PALM MUTING: The note is partially muted by the pick hand lightly touching the string(s) just before the bridge.

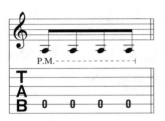

P.M. - - - - - - - - - - - - - - |

T
A
B
0   0   0   0

RAKE: Drag the pick across the strings indicated with a single motion.

rake - - - |

T
A
B
5
X

TREMOLO PICKING: The note is picked as rapidly and continuously as possible.

T
A
B
5   7

ARPEGGIATE: Play the notes of the chord indicated by quickly rolling them from bottom to top.

T
A
B
5
5
5
5

VIBRATO BAR DIVE AND RETURN: The pitch of the note or chord is dropped a specified number of steps (in rhythm) then returned to the original pitch.

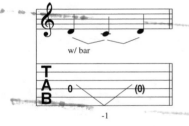

w/ bar

T
A
B
0   (0)

-1

VIBRATO BAR SCOOP: Depress the bar just before striking the note, then quickly release the bar.

w/ bar - - - - - - - - - - |

T
A
B
4   5   7

VIBRATO BAR DIP: Strike the note and then immediately drop a specified number of steps, then release back to the original pitch.

-1/2   -1/2   -1/2

w/ bar - - - - - - - - - - - - - |

-1/2   -1/2   -1/2

T
A
B
7   7   7

Additional Musical Definitions

 (accent) • Accentuate note (play it louder)

 (accent) • Accentuate note with great intensity

 (staccato) • Play the note short

⊓ • Downstroke

∨ • Upstroke

D.S. al Coda • Go back to the sign (%), then play until the measure marked "***To Coda***," then skip to the section labelled "***Coda***."

D.C. al Fine • Go back to the beginning of the song and play until the measure marked "***Fine***" (end).

Rhy. Fig. • Label used to recall a recurring accompaniment pattern (usually chordal).

Riff • Label used to recall composed, melodic lines (usually single notes) which recur.

Fill • Label used to identify a brief melodic figure which is to be inserted into the arrangement.

Rhy. Fill • A chordal version of a Fill.

tacet • Instrument is silent (drops out).

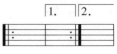 • Repeat measures between signs.

1. 2. • When a repeated section has different endings, play the first ending only the first time and the second ending only the second time.

NOTE: Tablature numbers in parentheses mean:
1. The note is being sustained over a system (note in standard notation is tied), or
2. The note is sustained, but a new articulation (such as a hammer-on, pull-off, slide or vibrato begins), or
3. The note is a barely audible "ghost" note (note in standard notation is also in parentheses).